Copyright © 2022 Matthew Douglas Pinard

All Rights Reserved. No part of this book publication may be reproduced or transmitted in any form or by any means, mechanical or electronic, including photocopying, scanning, and recording, or by any information storage and retrieval system, or other -- without prior permission in writing from the author or publisher. Disclaimers: The Publisher and the Author make no representation or warranties concerning the accuracy or completeness of the contents of this work and specifically disclaim all warranties for a particular purpose. No warranty may be created or extended through sales or promotional materials. The advice and strategies contained herein may not be suitable for every situation. This work is sold with the understanding that the Author and Publisher are not engaged in rendering legal, technological, or other professional services. If professional assistance is required, the services of a competent professional should be sought. Neither the Publisher nor the Author shall be liable for damages arising therefrom. The fact that an organization or website is referred to in this work as a citation and/or potential source of further information does not mean that the Author or the Publisher endorses the information, the organization, or website it may provide, or recommendations it may make. Further, readers should be aware that the websites listed in this work may have changed or disappeared between the time that this work was written and when it is read. Details of the cases and stories in this book have been changed to preserve privacy.

Printed in the United States of America

Published by: Writer's Publishing House
Prescott, Az 86301

Cover and Interior Design by Creative Artistic Excellence Marketing

Project Management and Book Launch by Creative Artistic Excellence Marketing https://lizzymcnett.com

Paperback ISBN: 978-1-64873-248-5
Hardcover ISBN: 978-1-64873-249-2
Ebook ISBN: 978-1-64873-251-5

Table of Contents

A YOUNG MAN HIKING — 11

A HALLOWEEN FOR THE AGES — 15

A BLUE BUTTERFLY — 36

JESUS CHRIST APPEARED — 41

HEALING OVER MY WIFE — 45

AN AMAZING TEACHER — 59

THE JOSHUA TREE — 66

SEVEN HORSES SEEM TO BE ON THE MARK — 83

THE STAR OF BETHLEHEM — 91

A CHRISTMAS TO REMEMBER — 100

THE ANGELS TAKE FLIGHT — 117

ANGELS TAKE FLIGHT — 118

THE FALLEN NINETEEN — 255

AN EXORCISING SUNSET — 314

SENDING ANGELS TO NEW FRIENDS — 356

ANGELS SENT — 363

AN EVER-APPROACHING APOCALYPSE — 370

THE DENVER INTERNATIONAL AIRPORT CONSPIRACY — 383

AN ANGEL IN MICHIGAN	*387*
ABOUT	*391*
THE	*391*
Other Books by Author Matthew Douglas Pinard	*392*
Screenplay Awards	*395*
Matthew Douglas Pinard	*395*

THE PRECIOUS Blood

The precious blood appeared literally out of nowhere. The day was Sunday, November 8, 2020 near St. George, Utah. The Extra Ordinary Minister of Holy Communion said prayers for the reception of the Eucharist, symbolizing the actual body and blood of our Lord Jesus Christ, and opened his Pyx to give communion to a sick parishioner.

The Pyx was full, as the Minister visited nineteen local area homes that Sunday to administer sacraments to the sick and infirmed. As the Minister carefully extracted one Host for the woman, another Host fell to the floor from the Pyx. The Minister carefully picked up the Host from the floor and placed the Host in his palm under the open Pyx, and distributed communion to the woman. He then placed the Pyx back into a burse and took out a folded handkerchief, and placed the Host that had fallen inside half of the handkerchief carefully folded into quarters. The Minister then folded the handkerchief again to about an eighth, so he could fit the handkerchief into his shirt pocket.

After visiting the rest of the parishioners and administering Holy Communion to each of them, the Extra Ordinary Minister went home around 2 p.m. In the Minister's house, there is a Crucifix and a candle on the fireplace mantle where he then consumed the dropped host placed inside the handkerchief. The Minister reached into his shirt pocket to find the Host and after doing so closed his eyes as he said the Lord's Prayer before consuming the Host. As the Extra Ordinary Minister opened the handkerchief with both hands to the half-unfolded portion, he immediately saw the entire handkerchief was covered in what would later be called the "precious blood."

The Extra Ordinary Minister was shocked, as he was a first-hand witness to what would later be investigated by the Roman Catholic Church as a precious blood miracle, a miraculous and undeniable physical manifestation of the blood of

Jesus Christ, our Lord and Savior. He immediately stopped consuming the fallen Host and took out a small bowl and placed the remaining three parts of the partially consumed Host into the bowl.

The Extra Ordinary Minister then placed the blood-soaked handkerchief containing the precious blood of Christ on top of the covered bowl, before making his way to Saint George Catholic Church to report this amazing miracle and to secure the bowl and handkerchief in the Church tabernacle to preserve the evidence for the Vatican. What was particularly interesting about this miracle was when it occurred. It happened on November 8th, 2020. That same day, my wife Carol Rose and I were just getting into the St. George, UT area due to my work there with local retina surgeons.

I do not find it coincidental as the author of The New Wine book series, which I believe is divinely inspired by St. Mary herself after witnessing an apparition of her in late 2016, that I was also chosen to bear witness to this apocalyptic type of miracle, possibly signaling the return of our True King. I was actually unaware of the miracle being investigated until mid-January 2021, when I returned to the St. George, UT area where I met a woman of incredible faith named Sheila, who approached me during a mass at St. George Catholic Church, where she handed me a photograph of the blood-soaked handkerchief, along with a statement written by the Extra Ordinary Minister of his experience.

Photo: While traveling to the St. George, Utah area to work with local retina surgeons I took this amazing photograph of the sun setting on the evening of November 8th, 2020 fully unaware of the precious blood miracle that was to take place that same day.

A YOUNG MAN HIKING

In early 2021, after working in the greater Las Vegas, NV area with local retina surgeons helping them focus with microscopes during surgery. I was driving along Interstate Route 15 when I saw young man hiking along the road. Now, I know what you are thinking. Only a crazy person would stop to try to help a hitchhiker. He's definitely dangerous, probably a serial killer or on drugs or looking to rob someone. Against this advice, I stopped to see if I could help this young man, having felt moved by the spirit to assist him.

After a brief discussion, this young man told me he was walking from Los Angeles, California all the way to Denver,

Colorado for his eight-year-old daughter's birthday celebration, over 1,000 miles, so as not to disappoint his daughter on her birthday.

After a brief discussion, he relayed a story where a young Mormon woman who was going to attend a church service was kind enough to let him sleep in her car while she and her daughters attended the service. I have to admit his outward appearance, which was quite goth with many facial tattoos, partially shaved head and worn-out pants and shirt, was a bit disconcerting. After speaking with him for five minutes I could determine he posed no threat.

This young man quickly opened up to me, telling me he was quite upset that he couldn't figure out where his life had gone wrong. He had once been enrolled in college and an Army ROTC program. I let him know I was an Army veteran. It was at this point of candidness that I noticed he had a Satanic ring on his left hand. It was a five star pentagram with an image of Satan as the Baphomet.

While I wanted to ask him how long he had been wearing the ring, and if his troubles started at that time, I refrained. He began to tell me he had spent many nights in jail and recently been brutally attacked and robbed after a night of heavy drinking in a West Hollywood bar.

He also had scars on his wrists from a suicide attempt, and relayed the story to me of lying in the bathtub full of blood near death, and feeling like he was floating before returning to his body. He was also a guitarist in a heavy metal band. In any event, I gave this young man a ride over two hours to the greater St. George, UT area, and left him near a gas station with a few dollars and some microwaved packets of food I had in my car. I wished him luck and told him not to give up in life. I think this is an experience that I will remember for quite some time.

It was frightening to think we are all one to two steps away from having real hardships and a very different life, and that sometimes who we serve spiritually can have a profound impact on the path we all take in this world. It was also a stark reminder that Satan and his fallen angels do not have our best interests in mind. In any event, it wasn't until the next day that I went inside St. George Catholic Church in St. George, UT to pray for this young man, that I ran into Sheila, who would inform me of the precious blood miracle being investigated by the Church.

Photo: This photograph was taken on January 24th, 2021 in the skies above St. George Catholic Church in St. George, UT where I met a woman of tremendous faith named Sheila who said she felt compelled after the mass to inform me of the precious blood miracle under investigation by the Catholic Church from November of 2020 which was during my last visit to the area to work with retina surgeons for my job. I see a winged Angel in flight that is also taking the form of a Holy Chalice or burse, yet another sign from on high that this truly was a miracle from heaven

A HALLOWEEN FOR THE AGES

Prior to the blood miracle in St. George, Utah on November 8th, 2020, we had a memorable Halloween in Prescott Valley, Arizona. This evening was extraordinary in terms of the incredible sunset and angel appearances as children trick or treat in our neighborhood. My wife and I had a low-key evening watching the old classic "Halloween" movie with Jamie Lee Curtis and Donald Pleasance. Our neighborhood hired a Sleepy Hollow themed "headless horseman" character to ride around the neighborhood, which I found to be incredibly cool.

Photo: The "headless horsemen" of Sleepy Hollow in our neighborhood the evening of October 30th, 2020 as our subdivision celebrated Halloween.

Photo: An incredibly beautiful angel forming over Prescott Valley, Arizona on October 30th, 2020 as we celebrated Halloween.

Photo: An incredible image of an angel hovering above a Church steeple Halloween October 30th, 2020 above Prescott Valley, Arizona.

Photo: An incredible image of a hovering angel above Prescott Valley, Arizona on October 30th, 2020.

Photo: An amazing hovering angel above Prescott Valley, Arizona on October 30th, 2020.

Photo: Yet another amazing angel over Prescott Valley, Arizona on October 30th, 2020 as we celebrated Halloween. The feathers and wings and bright blue orb are simply stunning.

Photo: Yet another amazing group of angels appearing above Prescott Valley, Arizona on October 30th, 2020 as our neighborhood celebrated Halloween.

Photo: An unmistakable angel in flight above Prescott Valley, Arizona as we celebrated Halloween on October 30th, 2020.

Photo: An enormous angelic looking face that appears to be grinning as it looks down on our neighborhood on October 30th, 2020 as we celebrated Halloween.

Photo: An incredibly beautiful angel in flight above Prescott Valley, Arizona on October 30th, 2020 as we celebrated Halloween. I see many hovering figures and faces in this angel network.

Photo: An amazing angel formation with multiple flying angels, crosses, and faces above Prescott Valley, Arizona on October 30th, 2020 as we celebrated Halloween.

Photo: Another amazing angel wing with a face in the middle of the frame above Prescott Valley, Arizona on October 30th, 2020 as we celebrated Halloween.

Photo: Yet another amazing angel formation the evening of October 30th, 2020 while celebrating Halloween in Prescott Valley, Arizona.

Photo: Another enormous angel directly above our home in Prescott Valley, Arizona on October 30th, 2020 as we celebrated Halloween.

Photo: As the sun was setting on October 30th, 2020 in Prescott Valley, Arizona this amazing angel face appeared at dusk in a beautiful orange and red hue. Can you see the cross on the top left?

Photo: The sunset soon morphed into this amazing orange wing covering the entire sky as the sun set on October 30th, 2020 after celebrating Halloween in our neighborhood in Prescott Valley, Arizona.

Photo: The incredible sunset above Prescott Valley, Arizona on October 30th, 2020 as we celebrated Halloween. Can you see the angel to the left with two beautiful wings?

Photo: Yet another shot of the amazing sunset the evening of October 30th, 2020 near Prescott Valley, Arizona as we celebrated Halloween in our subdivision with trick or treaters and a headless horseman.

Photo: Another amazing angelic sunset on October 31st, 2020 near Prescott Valley, Arizona as we celebrated Halloween.

Photo: Another amazing angelic sunset on October 31st, 2020 near Prescott Valley, Arizona as we celebrated Halloween.

A BLUE BUTTERFLY

On January 22, 2021 while on my way home from the greater Las Vegas, Nevada area after working with local retina surgeons, I had an incredible event occur around sunset that turned out to end up being the beginning of what I would call a miraculous healing event. As I was driving home a blue butterfly shape took form in the skies (I drew a blue line around the figure) right around sunset. I found the image to be quite odd, yet obviously a deliberate sign from the other kingdom.

Photo: An enormous blue butterfly shaped figure appeared in central Arizona on January 22, 2021 as I drove home from working near Las Vegas, NV with retina surgeons.

Photo: A lightened view of the enormous blue butterfly figure in the skies in central Arizona on January 22, 2021.

Photo: Another amazing image of a second blue butterfly like shaped figure in the skies near central Arizona on January 22, 2021 which I took again as confirmation of my call to pray for my wife to heal her from any trace of Hashimoto's disease.

Photo: On January 29th, 2021 this incredible image appeared directly above our home near Prescott Valley, Arizona. I had been praying daily for God the Father (Anunnaki Adonai) to heal my wife Carol Rose of thyroid disease. When I showed this photo to an Angel Group on Facebook that I am a part of they said, "I see the face of God."

Photo: On February 2nd, 2021 a third blue butterfly shaped figure appeared in the skies near central Arizona. I took this as a sign my prayers to heal my wife of Hashimoto's disease were heard.

JESUS CHRIST APPEARED

In this photo you can see the face of Christ looking down to the left of the frame. He is wearing his crown of thorns, and there appears to be blood dripping from his face onto a cross.

I had been praying for God to heal my wife of thyroid disease. To see the first Son's face was quite a relief and comforting. As I mentioned in previous volumes of The New Wine, I am his new wine and the third incarnation of The Son.

Photo: An incredible photograph of Jesus Christ appeared above Prescott Valley, Arizona near St. Germaine's Catholic Church on February 9th, 2021

Photo: On February 10th, 2021 yet another blue butterfly shaped image appeared directly above our home in Prescott Valley, Arizona. This was yet more confirmation my prayers for my wife's thyroid disease were heard by the other kingdom.

Photo: A statue of St. Mary inside St. Germaine's Catholic Church in Prescott Valley, Arizona. This is the very statue I sat in front of while I prayed for healing over my wife of any and all trace of thyroid disease on February 10th, 2021.

HEALING OVER MY WIFE

The incredible appearance of the large blue butterfly shaped figure became apparent soon after. The exact day this image appeared, my wife called me to inform me that her physician had run some blood tests, and she was told she had the early stages of Hashimoto's disease.

The curious thing about Hashimoto's disease is that the body's own immune system attacks the thyroid gland and causes hormonal imbalances, which can wreak havoc on the body. Interestingly enough, the thyroid gland is also called the "butterfly gland."

After finding the appearance of this blue butterfly shaped image in the skies was not coincidental, I took it as a sign from God that I should pray over my wife to heal her from this debilitating disease.

That same evening, I took some Holy Water and said the following prayer,

"Ashanti Anunnaki Adonai, Ashanti Anunnaki Angel, Ashanti Anunnaki Sancti, please heal your yellow rose, heal your Carol Rose Kloss of all diseases of the butterfly gland."

As I placed Holy Water on my wife's throat. Amazingly enough, two months later, my wife Carol Rose went to the same physician, who after running new blood tests could find no trace of any Hashimoto's or pre-Hashimoto's thyroid disease.

TWO HEARTS BEAT AS ONE

My wife Carol Rose and I have a good friend named Sherri who lives in Prescott, Arizona. Sherri is a loving down home southern girl from Arkansas with one of the best accents I've ever heard.

Sherri, like many others, was a victim of the COVID-19 virus that left her with a heart aneurysm which is a small ballooning of a major heart artery that can lead to a fatal stroke.

After Sherri started having serious chest pains and was scheduled to undergo a stress test in April of 2021. I offered to pray with Sherri just as I had with my wife. Sherri was incredibly open minded and had no reservations about trying to heal her heart condition through prayers.

I met Sherri on Saturday, April 24th, 2021 at Sacred Heart Catholic Church in Prescott, Arizona. We both stood in front of the St. Mary statue. As we touched Mary's hands, we placed our other hands together and said the following prayers,

"Ashanti Anunnaki Adonai, Ashanti Anunnaki Angel, Ashanti Anunnaki Sancti, Mary please heal Sherri's heart, remove any trace of disease from her and as a sign that we have been heard please show us in the skies today many angels and also show us a four chambered heart as a sign that we have been heard."

We then said three Hail Mary's. On a day with absolutely no clouds in the skies the following images appeared.

Photo: The first of many angel wings appears in the skies above Prescott, Arizona on April 24th, 2021 after prayers at a local Catholic Church.

Photo: Another large angel wing appears above Prescott, Arizona on April 24th, 2021 after saying prayers at a local Catholic Church with a good friend named Sherri who had a serious heart condition as a result of complications from COVID-1

Photo: Another set of large angel wings appears above Prescott, Arizona on April 24th, 2021 after saying prayers at a local Catholic Church with a good friend named Sherri who had a serious heart condition as a result of complications from COVID-19.

Photo: Another set of large angel wings appears above Prescott, Arizona on April 24th, 2021 after saying prayers at a local Catholic Church with a good friend named Sherri who had a serious heart condition as a result of complications from COVID-19.

Photo: Another large angel wing appears above Prescott, Arizona on April 24th, 2021 after saying prayers at a local Catholic Church with a good friend named Sherri who had a serious heart condition as a result of complications from COVID-19.

Photo: Another large angel wing appears at sunset above Prescott, Arizona on April 24th, 2021 after saying prayers at a local Catholic Church with a good friend named Sherri who had a serious heart condition as a result of complications from COVID-19.

Photo: Another large angel wing appears at sunset above Prescott, Arizona on April 24th, 2021 after saying prayers at a local Catholic Church with a good friend named Sherri who had a serious heart condition as a result of complications from COVID-19.

Photo: Another large angel wing appears at sunset above Prescott, Arizona on April 24th, 2021 directly above the apartment complex where our friend Sherri lives after saying prayers at a local Catholic Church for her serious heart condition as a result of complications from COVID-19

Photo: Another large angel wing appears at sunset above Prescott, Arizona on April 24th, 2021 after saying prayers at a local Catholic Church with a good friend named Sherri who had a serious heart condition as a result of complications from COVID-19.

Photo: Another large angel wing appears at sunset above Prescott, Arizona on April 24th, 2021 after saying prayers at a local Catholic Church with a good friend named Sherri who had a serious heart condition as a result of complications from COVID-19.

Photo: Another large angel wing appears at sunset above Prescott, Arizona on April 24th, 2021 after saying prayers at a local Catholic Church with a good friend named Sherri who had a serious heart condition as a result of complications from COVID-19.

Photo: Another large angel wing appears at sunset above Prescott, Arizona on April 24th, 2021 after saying prayers at a local Catholic Church with a good friend named Sherri who had a serious heart condition as a result of complications from COVID-19.

Photo: Another large angel wing appears at sunset above Prescott, Arizona on April 24th, 2021 after saying prayers at a local Catholic Church with a good friend named Sherri who had a serious heart condition as a result of complications from COVID-19.

Photo: A very large four chambered heart appears above Prescott, Arizona on April 24th, 2021 after saying prayers at a local Catholic Church with a good friend named Sherri who had a serious heart condition as a result of complications from COVID-19.

Photo: A second very four chambered heart appears above Prescott, Arizona on April 24th, 2021 after saying prayers at a local Catholic Church with a good friend named Sherri who had a serious heart condition as a result of complications from COVID-19.

On Sunday May 9th, 2021 I texted our friend Sherri who after passing with flying colors a heart stress test (the cardiologist could find no evidence of remaining disease and chose not to complete a nuclear dye test because her test was so positive), Sherri replied with a text and this photo below which she took while praying outdoors during a hike. The photo shows a backwards hovering large "S" for Sherri above a heart shaped cloud.

AN AMAZING TEACHER

On January 12, 2021, the world lost an incredible teacher and spirit after a man named Terry Ernest Caputo passed away following an extended illness. Terry was my eighth-grade basketball coach and also an incredibly passionate teacher who taught at Huron Valley Christian School in Ypsilanti, Michigan.

As I mentioned in the first volume of The New Wine, my fraternal twin James Douglas Morrison and I once wrote that "death makes angels of us all and gives us wings where we had shoulders smooth as raven's claws." This was soon going to be quite apparent to me, as I received multiple signs in the skies that Terry was now just that, an angel looking over all of us, following his death.

OBITUARY

Terry Ernest Caputo

AUGUST 10, 1952 – JANUARY 12, 2021

Terry Ernest Caputo, 68, of Ypsilanti, MI, peacefully passed away on January 12th surrounded by loved ones, after an extended illness.

Photo: On January 16th, 2021 this incredibly beautiful angel wing appeared at sunrise near Prescott Valley, Arizona while on my way to pray for Terry Caputo, an old teacher and coach from my youth

Photo: While praying for the repose of the soul of a former teacher and coach Terry Caputo this amazingly beautiful angel wing appeared at sunset on January 22nd, 2021.

Photo: On January 22nd, 2021 an incredible image of what appears as a large Liberty Bell appeared in the skies near Prescott Valley, Arizona. This was right after an old teacher and coach named Terry Caputo had passed away on to bigger and better things to do for the other kingdom.

Photo: An amazingly beautiful angel face staring down appeared on January 22nd, 2021 near Prescott Valley, Arizona following the death of a former teacher and coach Terry Caputo.

Photo: On January 23rd, 2021 this beautiful angel wing appeared above St. Germaine Catholic Church in Prescott Valley, Arizona while on my way to say a rosary for the soul of a former teacher and coach Terry Caputo.

Photo: An incredible image of an angel in flight above Sacred Heart Catholic Church in Prescott, Arizona the morning of January 24th, 2021 on the day of the funeral for Terry Caputo, an old coach and teacher from my youth. I had prayed an entire rosary for Terry that morning and this image appeared directly above the church immediately after.

Photo: On January 24th, 2021 the exact date of the funeral celebration for Terry Caputo another amazing angel wing appeared at sunset in honor of Terry's life of service to others.

THE JOSHUA TREE

The amazing band U2 saw the Joshua Tree in Joshua Tree National Park as a symbol of faith and hope in that springs forth in an arid climate.

Joshua Trees grows fiercely in adverse conditions and it was named after the Mormon Prophet Joshua after the branches on the tree reminded settlers of the Prophet Joshua raising his arms in prayers. When the Prophet Matthew Douglas Pinard (The New Wine) visited with his amazingly spiritual powerful wife Carol Rose Kloss (The New Rose) quite a few amazing angel events occurred in the skies. The evening of January 3rd, 2021 gave us a glimpse of the amazing views we would see the next day at Joshua Tree National Park in Joshua Tree, California.

Photo: The sunset near Joshua Tree, California in January 3rd, 2021 as we traveled to visit the incredible national park named after the Mormon Prophet Joshua.

Photo: The sunrise the morning of January 4th, 2021 near Joshua Tree National Park in Joshua Tree, California was unlike any I've ever seen. The pink clouds were incredibly mysterious as the sun rose. I know it was going to be a day filled with angel sightings.

Photo: Another shot of the sunrise near Joshua Tree, California on January 4th, 2021. The pink clouds reflecting sunlight with the bright moon in the distance is simply breathtaking.

Photo: Another amazing view of the sunrise the morning of January 4th, 2021 as we prepared to visit Joshua Tree National Park in California. You can clearly see what appears to be angel wings above the trees.

Photo: An amazing angel in flight near Joshua Tree, California the morning of January 4th, 2021 as we waited nearby patiently for roadside assistance from a blown tire on our recreational vehicle. This angel is flying from right to left towards the sun arms outstretched.

Photo: An incredible pair of angel wings hovering above Joshua trees in Joshua Tree National Park on January 4th, 2021 as my wife Carol and I visited for the first time.

Photo: An incredible face and towering angelic figure inside of Joshua Tree National Park in California on January 4th, 2021.

Photo: An incredible photo of what appears to be a diving angel from inside Joshua Tree National Park in California as we visited on January 4th, 2021.

Photo: An amazing angel in flight (from left to right) in the skies above Joshua Tree, California on January 4th, 2021.

Photo: An absolutely stunning image of an angel with a cross flying above Joshua Tree National Park, California on January 4th, 2021.

Photo: An incredible photo from January 4th, 2021 shows a large angel to the right as a smaller angel hover to the left of the large angel above Joshua Tree National Park, California.

Photo: An incredible photo of an angel face from January 4th, 2021 in Joshua Tree National Park, California.

Photo: An incredible grouping of hovering angels on January 4th, 2021 above Joshua Tree National Park, California.

Photo: An incredible angel wing on January 4th, 2021 in Joshua Tree National Park, California.

Photo: An amazing photo of what appears to be two conjoined fraternal twin angels in flight, however, each moving in the opposite direction away from each other on January 4th, 2021 inside Joshua Tree National Park in California. I find this to be quite representative of the current state of the world in which even the closest of family members are moving away from each other in division which is an instrument of the devil.

Photo: An amazing image of a hovering angel sitting down working on something, possibly typing something the evening of January 4th, 2021 as my wife and I made our way home from Joshua Tree, California.

Photo: An amazing image of a large buffalo head in the skies above central Arizona on January 4th, 2021 as my wife and I made our way home from Joshua Tree, California. This for me was confirmation the other kingdom recognizes my favorite animal is the buffalo as evidenced by my poem from The New Wine Volume II: Peace Town entitled "Buffalo."

SEVEN HORSES SEEM TO BE ON THE MARK

In The Doors song "Love Her Madly" the left jaw of St. Mary, James Douglas Morrison, my fraternal twin and half-brother sings "seven horses seem to be on the mark."

I've listened to this song hundreds of times and for some reason this lyric seemed odd and out of place. However, I now believe this to be incredibly prophetic of seven horses of the Apocalypse that would appear in our skies during a time of great turmoil. These seven horses would also appear following the pass of Nibiru and its seven orbiting planets brining many thousands of Angels from other kingdom along with it to try to save the human race. I've now captured what I deem to be the seven horses as I will document below with photographs.

Photo: The first "horse" of the apocalypse appearing above Sacred Heart Catholic Church in Prescott, Arizona on June 16th, 2020. You can clearly see a horse head with eye and mouth in this frame.

Photo: The second "horse" of the apocalypse appeared above Prescott, Arizona on July 13th, 2020. You can clearly see a horse head with ears, eyes and mouth.

Photo: The third "horse" of the apocalypse appeared above Prescott, Arizona on October 30th, 2020 the day before Halloween. The horse head is in the middle of the frame.

Photo: The fourth "horse" of the apocalypse appeared on December 7th, 2020 which strangely was also the same date as the bombing of Pearl Harbor in 1941 which brought the United States fully into World War II. This horse head is a bit more subtle but in the model of the frame with eye and mouth.

Photo: The fifth "horse "of the apocalypse appeared on January 12th, 2021 above Prescott, Arizona. This horse is pretty clear in the lower middle left of the frame with an eye and nose in view.

Photo: The sixth "horse "of the apocalypse appeared at sunset on January 15th, 2021 above Prescott Valley, Arizona. The head is looking to the right and is in the top middle right of the frame.

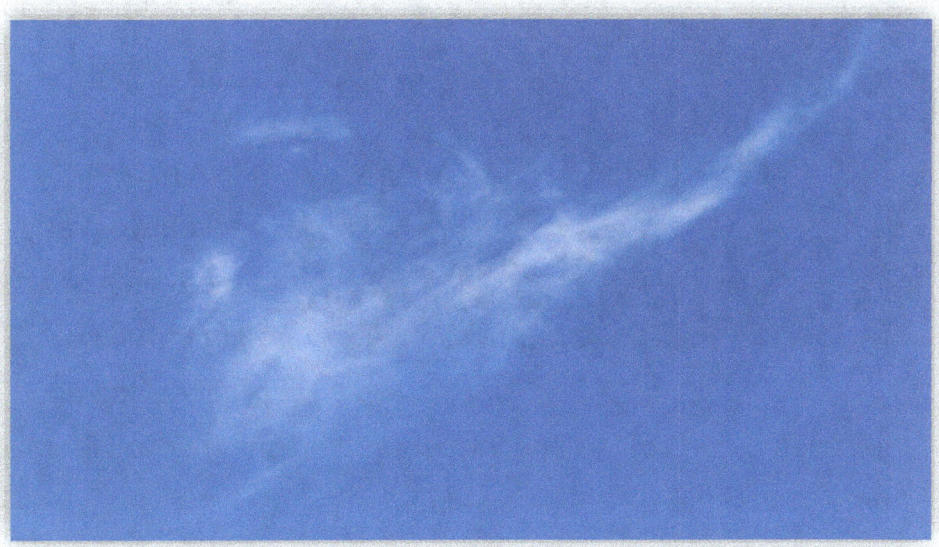

Photo: The seventh and final "horse" of the apocalypse can be found in the skies above Prescott Valley, Arizona on March 2nd, 2021 and is fairly clear with eyes and nose in the middle left of the frame.

Photo: An undated photograph of the left jaw of St. Mary, Son of God, James Douglas Morrison prior to his "death" in 1971. James was a prophet as well as an amazing and prophetic poet and musical lyricist. I was with him his entire life and have many memories of his life including prophesying about the seven horses of the apocalypse with the song Love Her Madly from 1971 on the L.A. Woman album.

Photo: The right jaw of St. Mary and reincarnation of James Douglas Morrison as Matthew Douglas Pinard in 2020.

James knew and I would be alive together in 2020-2021 to witness the seven horses of the apocalypse that we prophesied would appear from the song Love Her Madly off the L.A. Woman album from 1971.

As for my own spiritual identity I will answer that with three examples. The first example is the Catholic Priest from St. Mary's Catholic Church in Spring Lake, Michigan who said to his congregation while I was still an active parishioner there "you may have seen Jesus' walking into church this morning" on a Sunday I was at that service, or the other Catholic Priest from Cottonwood, Arizona who said after reading my books that I am a Mystic. You could also ask one of the women who felt compelled to pray with me at St. Mary's Catholic Church in Spring Lake, Michigan who said she saw the Holy Eucharist covered in light floating above my forehead as she prayed.

THE STAR OF BETHLEHEM

On December 21st, 2020 a conjunction of Jupiter and Saturn in the skies that has not been seen since the Star of Bethlehem that the three wisemen followed on their quest to find the Christ child.

This star was incredibly brilliant and bright and appeared to many across the entire planet. I was also able to witness and to take photographs of numerous powerful supernatural events just prior to this date, on the actual date and a few days after.

Some of these images are some of the most powerful I've ever witnessed and were confirmation that this astral alignment holds great significance for the earth.

Photo: The Star of Bethlehem as Jupiter and Saturn re-aligned on December 21st, 2020.

Photo: Ten days prior to the Star of Bethlehem sighting, this incredibly powerful image of the face of Satan can be seen in the sunset in central Arizona on December 11th, 2020.

Photo: An incredible photograph of angels gathering above St. Thomas Catholic Church in Tucson, Arizona on December 21st, 2020 the day the Star of Bethlehem would appear in the night sky.

Photo: Angels hovering above Corpus Christi Catholic Church in Tucson, Arizona on December 21st, 2020 the same day Saturn and Jupiter would align forming a new Star of Bethlehem.

Photo: An angel in flight in central Arizona on December 21st, 2020 the day the Star of Bethlehem would appear in our skies during a rare alignment of Jupiter and Saturn.

Photo: An amazing image of lightning striking an erupting volcano on December 21st, 2020 the day Saturn and Jupiter would align forming an astral event not seen since the Star of Bethlehem.

Photo: The morning of December 22nd, 2020 brought with it an incredible image at sunrise near Tucson, Arizona. This is a rare sighting of St. Michael the Taxi Arch Angel flying sideways in the sunset a wing pointed towards the ground.

Photo: Another amazing image of the sunrise near Tucson, Arizona on December 22nd, 2020 the morning after the world witnessed Saturn and Jupiter aligning in the night skies, an event not seen since the birth of Christ and the Star of Bethlehem. This photo shows an amazing image of a demonic looking face in the sunrise. I am taking this image as an exorcism of this demonic fallen entity from this earth.

Photo: A few days after the Star of Bethlehem reappeared in our skies for the

first time in over two thousand years as Jupiter and Saturn aligned this incredible photograph shows the northern lights of the aurora borealis forming in the shape of a flying angel in the sky on December 24th, 2020.

A CHRISTMAS TO REMEMBER

The week of Christmas 2020 was one to remember as we witnessed multiple angel sightings in central Arizona. This Christmas was notable for the return appearance of the Christmas Star as also documented in this book which is an amazing alignment of Jupiter and Saturn in the night skies in late December 2020.

Photo: On December 21st, 2020 as the Star of Bethlehem was set to make its first appearance in over two thousand years this choir of angels hovered above St. Thomas Catholic Church in Tucson, Arizona where I said a rosary for world peace and for the world to turn away from war and greed.

Photo: On December 22nd, 2020 this amazingly beautiful pair of angel wings appeared near Tucson, Arizona.

Photo: On December 25th, 2020 Christmas Day this beautiful angel hovered in the skies near central Arizona soon after the appearance of the Star of Bethlehem.

Photo: On December 25th, 2020 Christmas Day this beautiful angel hovered in the skies near central Arizona soon after the appearance of the Star of Bethlehem right above the steeple at St. Germaine Catholic Church.

Photo: On December 26th, 2020 this beautiful angel hovered in the skies near central Arizona soon after the appearance of the Star of Bethlehem.

Photo: On December 26th, 2020 this beautiful angel hovered in the skies near central Arizona soon after the appearance of the Star of Bethlehem.

Photo: On December 26th, 2020 these two beautiful angels hovered in the skies near central Arizona soon after the appearance of the Star of Bethlehem. It appears as if they are having some kind of angel conference.

Photo: On December 26th, 2020 this beautiful angel danced and glided above the skies near central Arizona soon after the appearance of the Star of Bethlehem.

Photo: On December 27th, 2020 this beautiful angel hovered in the skies near central Arizona soon after the appearance of the Star of Bethlehem. You can see this angel appears to be looking down to the left of frame.

Photo: On December 27th, 2020 this beautiful angel in the shape of a cross hovered in the skies near central Arizona soon after the appearance of the Star of Bethlehem.

Photo: On December 27th, 2020 these beautiful hovering angels in the shape

of a crosses hovered in the skies near central Arizona soon after the appearance of the Star of Bethlehem.

Photo: On December 27th, 2020 this beautiful angel hovered in the skies near central Arizona soon after the appearance of the Star of Bethlehem.

Photo: On December 27th, 2020 this beautiful angel hovered in the skies near central Arizona soon after the appearance of the Star of Bethlehem.

Photo: On December 27th, 2020 this beautiful angel hovered in the skies near central Arizona soon after the appearance of the Star of Bethlehem.

Photo: On December 27th, 2020 this beautiful angel hovered in the skies near central Arizona soon after the appearance of the Star of Bethlehem. You can see a huge face to the top middle of the frame holding out a left arm or wing.

Photo: On December 27th, 2020 this beautiful angel hovered in the skies near central Arizona soon after the appearance of the Star of Bethlehem. You can see two wings in the middle of the frame.

Photo: On December 27th, 2020 this beautiful angel hovered in the skies near central Arizona soon after the appearance of the Star of Bethlehem.

Photo: On December 27th, 2020 this beautiful angel hovered in the skies near central Arizona soon after the appearance of the Star of Bethlehem.

On December 29th, 2020 a local man named Steven "Woody" Woodham passed away in Phoenix, Arizona. I had happened to stop by his memorial service at St. Germaine Catholic Church in Prescott Valley, Arizona and noticed something quite extraordinary. By all accounts Steven was not only an accomplished musician loved by many, but also a man of great Catholic faith. The sunset photos from the actual date of his passing are seen below and are quite incredible.

Photo: An incredibly mysterious sunset the evening of December 29th, 2020 above Prescott Valley, Arizona after a local man of musical talent and faith Steven "Woody" Woodham passed away in central Arizona.

Photo: An amazing photo of the setting sun and a huge ray of red light shooting upwards toward heaven on December 29th, 2020 the same day an accomplished musician and a man of great faith named Steven "Woody" Woodham passed away in central Arizona.

ANGELS TAKE FLIGHT

Photo: This enormous angel wing covered the entire sky on August 8th, 2020 near Prescott Valley, Arizona. The spiritual energy that emanated from this wing was as powerful as anything I've ever experienced.

Photo: The evening of August 20th, 2020 shows an incredibly mysterious sunset with a strange looking face near the middle of the frame staring directly at the camera above Prescott Valley, Arizona.

Photo: This beautiful angel appeared above Prescott Valley, Arizona on August 21st, 2020 after a saying a rosary at Sacred Heart Catholic Church in Prescott, Arizona. The wing coming over the top is simply beautiful.

Photo: The evening sunset of August 23rd, 2021 above Prescott Valley, Arizona shows an incredible image of what appears to be a figure looking to the right near the bottom right of the frame with two wing tips behind the figure near the top left of the frame.

Photo: This angel flying sideways on September 7th, 2020 above Prescott Valley, Arizona was quite clearly a messenger from the other kingdom showing off his flight skills.

Photo: On September 21st, 2020 this very mysterious eye appeared in the skies above Prescott Valley, Arizona. It appears to me almost as an all-seeing eye.

Photo: The sunset on September 24th, 2020 brought this incredibly mysterious cloud above Prescott Valley, Arizona. If you look closely enough you can see a demonic looking face being exorcised into the clouds by larger more powerful angels.

Photo: This incredible photo above Prescott Valley, Arizona on October 5th, 2020 shows what appears to be a floating King's crown in the sky. More confirmation the True King is on the earth to enact change.

Photo: A choir of hovering angels over Phoenix, Arizona on October 7th, 2020. This image is breathtakingly beautiful beyond words.

Photo: One of the most clear angel photographs I've ever taken on October 8th, 2020 above Prescott Valley, Arizona. This female angel is so beautiful and you can clearly see her legs and arms and head with two wings in flight.

Photo: On October 8th, 2020 this incredible angel was seen hovering above a mural of Jesus Christ in the Garden of Stone at St. Germaine Catholic Church in Prescott Valley, Arizona.

Photo: On October 8th, 2020 this beautiful angel took flight above Prescott Valley, Arizona.

Photo: On October 9th, 2020 this amazing twin headed angel was found hovering in the skies above our home in Prescott Valley, Arizona. It is a simply stunning image of an entity from the other kingdom.

Photo: An incredible set of huge angel wings above St. Germaine Catholic Church on October 21st, 2020 in Prescott Valley, Arizona.

Photo: An incredibly angelic sunset above Prescott Valley, Arizona on October 21st, 2020 shows multiple angelic entities hovering in protection above our hometown.

Photo: On October 21st, 2020 this incredibly beautiful angel wing covered the entire sky above Prescott Valley, Arizona.

Photo: On October 21st, 2020 this large angel wing morphed into something quite beautiful and amazing above Prescott Valley, Arizona.

Photo: Another amazing view of angels in flight above Prescott Valley, Arizona on October 21st, 2020.

Photo: Another amazing view of angels in flight on October 21st, 2020 above Prescott Valley, Arizona.

Photo: An incredible view of an angel in flight on October 21st, 2020 near Prescott Valley, Arizona. There is a definite face near the top of the frame.

Photo: On October 21st, 2020 this incredibly beautiful angel with multiple wings took flight above Prescott Valley, Arizona.

Photo: On October 21st, 2020 this amazingly beautiful angel can be seen just to the left of the sun above Prescott Valley, Arizona. You can clearly see a head, chest, and two wings folded outwards in flight.

Photo: On October 21st, 2020 this incredible photograph has captured what I believe to be the face of our True King and first Son Jesus Christ above Prescott Valley, Arizona. You can see his face in the top middle of the frame and there is a cross below his face. There is also an angel just to the right of the frame holding its wings up and facing Christ protecting him.

Photo: An amazing photo of what appears to be an angel hovering and folding its hands in prayer above Prescott Valley, Arizona on October 21st, 2020.

Photo: Another amazing photo of an angel hovering on October 21st, 2020 above Prescott Valley, Arizona and its hand up to its face with a rather inquisitive look almost like "what shall I do next?"

Photo: An incredible image of an angel sitting on top of a cloud its wings behind its back as it hovers above Prescott Valley, Arizona on October 21st, 2020.

Photo: An amazing image of an large angel face in the skies above Prescott Valley, Arizona on October 21st, 2020.

Photo: Another angelic face hovering above Prescott Valley, Arizona on October 21st, 2020.

Photo: An incredible image of an angel hovering in flight over a demon in the skies above Prescott Valley, Arizona on October 21st, 2020.

Photo: More angels in flight hovering above Prescott Valley, Arizona on October 21st, 2020.

Photo: An incredible image of what appears to be an eye in the middle of the frame surround by more angel wings on October 21st, 2020 above Prescott Valley, Arizona

Photo: Yet another angel in flight with a face in the middle of the frame above Prescott Valley, Arizona on October 21st, 2020.

Photo: An amazing angel in flight above Prescott Valley, Arizona in October 21st, 2020.

Photo: An incredible angel in flight that appears to be looking over its right shoulder above Prescott Valley, Arizona on October 21st, 2020.

Photo: An army of angels in flight directly above the roof of our home in Prescott Valley, Arizona on October 21st, 2020.

Photo: A pair of very mysterious angelic eyes staring down from the skies above Prescott Valley, Arizona on October 21st, 2020.

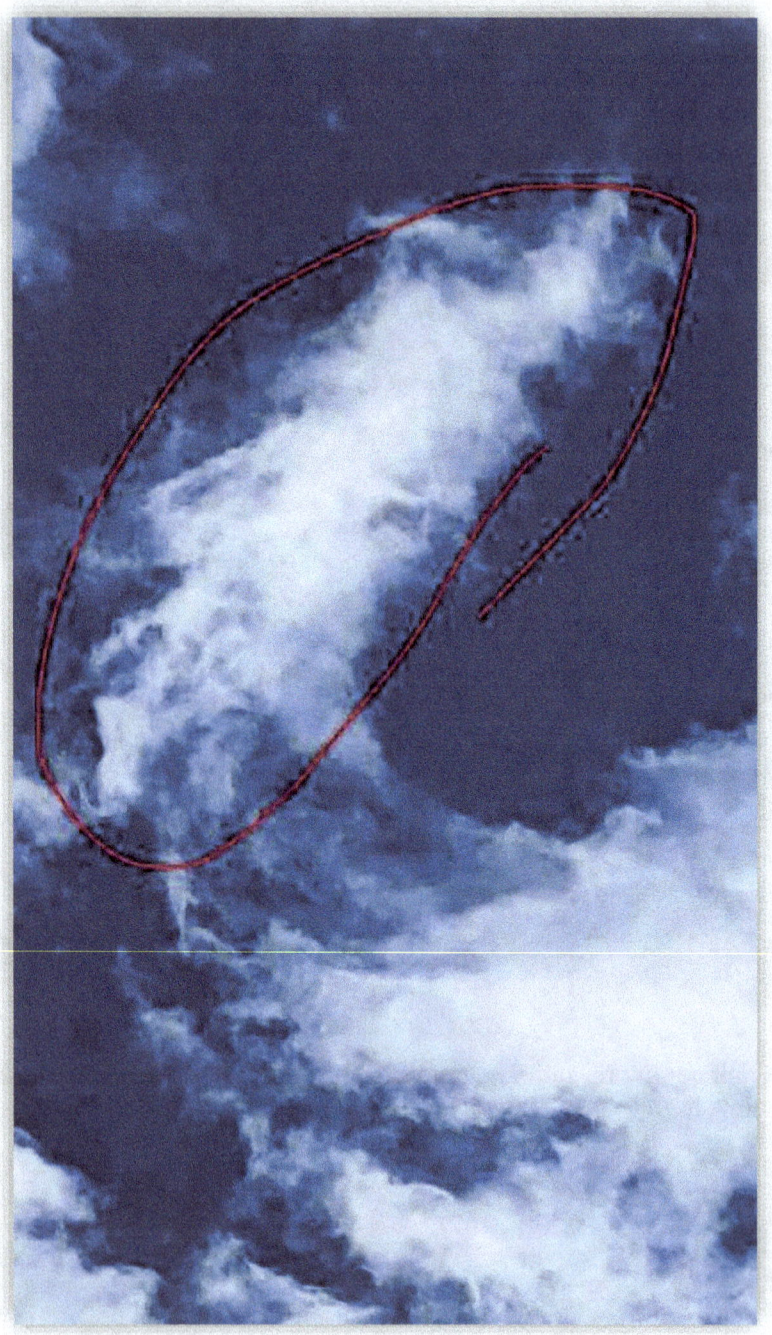

Photo: Another angel face to the top left hovering in flight above Prescott Valley, Arizona on October 21st, 2020.

Photo: An amazing angel in flight near the sun above Prescott Valley, Arizona on October 21st, 2020.

Photo: An incredible angel wing hovers above the sun near Prescott Valley, Arizona on October 23rd, 2020.

Photo: An incredible angel face looking to the left as it hovers over Prescott Valley, Arizona on October 23rd, 2020.

Photo: An incredibly beautiful sunset reveals a demonic looking face the evening of October 23rd, 2020 near Prescott Valley, Arizona.

Photo: On October 24th, 2020 we spent a night camping with some friends near Flagstaff, Arizona and this incredibly mysterious cloud formed right above Humphrey's Peak. I jokingly said I would not be surprised if a UFO flew out of the could the image was so compelling.

Photo: This incredible image of an angel hovering in flight wings spread was taken on October 26th, 2020 above Prescott Valley, Arizona.

Photo: The morning of October 26th, 2020 brought an amazing sunrise as I headed to St. Germaine Catholic Church in Prescott Valley, Arizona for a morning rosary. If you look closely enough you can see a cross to the right above the clouds backlit by sun.

Photo: The sunrise of October 26th, 2020 brought this amazing image of a cross backlit by the rising sun near Prescott Valley, Arizona.

Photo: On November 1st, 2020 this incredible hovering angel was seen above a local church steeple in Prescott Valley, Arizona.

Photo: On November 1st, 2020 this amazing hovering angel was seen directly above the steeple at St. Germaine Catholic Church in Prescott Valley, Arizona.

Photo: On November 1st, 2020 this incredible wing was above the Garden of Stone at St. Germaine Catholic Church in Prescott Valley, Arizona. This place reminds of the Pearl Jam song "Garden of Stone" with the incredible lyrics, "I will walk with my hands bound into your garden, garden of stone" as sung by the Prophet Eddie Vedder (Edward Louis Severson).

Photo: On November 1st, 2020 this incredible feathered wing appeared above Prescott Valley, Arizona.

Photo: On November 1st, 2020 this amazing wing also appeared above Prescott Valley, Arizona.

Photo: On November 1st, 2020 the above angel appeared with an unmistakable smiling face near the top of the feather/wing above Prescott Valley, Arizona. It is simply beautiful and powerful to see this messenger from the other kingdom up close.

Photo: On November 2nd, 2020 this amazing face showed up in the sky which to me appears to me like a demonic face being exorcised up into the skies by an angel above Prescott Valley, Arizona

Photo: On November 3rd, 2020 these two huge "walking" angels appeared above Prescott Valley, Arizona on my way to Sacred Heart Catholic Church to do a rosary for world peace, for the world to disarm and turn away from greed.

Photo: On November 3rd, 2020 this amazing angel face appeared above Prescott Valley, Arizona while on my way to Sacred Heart Catholic Church for a morning rosary.

Photo: On November 3rd, 2020 this amazing angel arm and head appeared to effortlessly float above Prescott, Arizona after a morning rosary at Sacred Heart Catholic Church.

Photo: On November 3rd, 2020 this incredibly mysterious and very apocalyptic cloud appeared directly above my home in Prescott Valley, Arizona after a morning rosary at Sacred Heart Catholic Church.

Photo: On November 3rd, 2020 after a morning rosary at Sacred Heart Catholic Church in Prescott, Arizona this amazing winged angel cloud appeared directly above our home in Prescott Valley, Arizona.

Photo: If you look closely here you might see what appears to be two angels having a conference above Prescott Valley, Arizona the morning of November 3rd, 2020.

Photo: On November 3rd, 2020 this amazing angel flying was captured above Prescott Valley, Arizona.

Photo: On November 3rd, 2020 this incredible and mysterious face appeared above Prescott Valley, Arizona.

Photo: An incredible image of a hovering angel in the form of a cross as I recited a full rosary for world peace near an image of the first Son Jesus Christ in the band Pearl Jam's Garden of Stone at St. Germaine Catholic Church on November 3rd, 2020 near Prescott Valley, Arizona.

Photo: An incredible angel in flight above Prescott Valley, Arizona on November 3rd, 2020.

Photo: A very mysterious image of an angel in flight above Prescott Valley, Arizona on November 3rd, 2020.

Photo: An incredibly mysterious and beautiful angelic looking cloud above Prescott Valley, Arizona on November 3rd, 2020.

Photo: Another incredibly mysterious and beautiful angelic looking cloud above Prescott Valley, Arizona on November 3rd, 2020.

Photo: Another incredibly mysterious and beautiful angelic looking cloud above Prescott Valley, Arizona near sunset on November 3rd, 2020.

Photo: On November 6th, 2020 this mysterious cross appeared in the skies above Prescott Valley, Arizona after a morning rosary for world peace.

Photo: On November 6th, 2020 this hovering angel in flight also appeared above Prescott Valley, Arizona after a morning rosary for world peace.

Photo: On November 17th, 2020 these two huge angel wings appeared in the skies above Prescott Valley, Arizona.

Photo: On November 17th, 2020 this incredibly angelic looking face appeared above the skies near Prescott Valley, Arizona.

Photo: On November 21st, 2020 this amazing hovering angel face appeared above Prescott Valley, Arizona.

Photo: On November 21st, 2020 this incredible image of two angels face to face almost kissing appeared above Prescott Valley, Arizona. This is a beautiful image of celestial beings trying to direct this world to "Be Love."

Photo: The evening of November 21st, 2020 at sunset saw this huge dark wing appeared in the skies. It is hauntingly beautiful.

Photo: Taken on November 23rd, 2020 this incredible photograph shows an angelic figure looking down toward the left with an almost sad appearance. The figure seems to be holding its arms out and at the end of the arms or wings are two heads/faces.

Photo: On November 23rd, 2020 this incredible photograph shows angels hovering in the skies above Prescott Valley, Arizona.

Photo: The sunset above Prescott Valley, Arizona on November 23rd, 2020 was incredibly bright and orange and red and one of the most beautiful sunsets I have ever seen anywhere.

Photo: On November 30th, 2020 this incredible angelic looking cloud formed above Prescott Valley, Arizona.

Photo: On November 30th, 2020 another incredible angelic looking cloud formed above Prescott Valley, Arizona.

Photo: On November 30th, 2020 yet another incredible angelic looking cloud formed above Prescott Valley, Arizona.

Photo: On November 30th, 2020 yet another incredible angelic looking cloud formed above Prescott Valley, Arizona.

Photo: On November 30th, 2020 yet another incredible angelic looking cloud formed above Prescott Valley, Arizona. Notice the blue/green orb bottom center of the frame right below what appears to be an angelic face looking down to the right.

Photo: On December 1st, 2020 this red dancing angel appeared in the skies near dusk above Prescott Valley, Arizona. The body of the angel is unmistakable.

Photo: On December 1st, 2020 this incredible angel wing also appeared above Prescott Valley, Arizona.

Photo: On December 6th, 2020 near the Garden of Stone at St. Germaine Catholic Church in Prescott Valley, Arizona this incredible triple angel wing appeared right above where Jesus Christ and his Apostles are symbolically holding the last supper in stone artwork along the garden wall.

Photo: On December 6th, 2020 above St. Germaine Catholic Church in Prescott Valley, Arizona you can see an amazing hovering angel right above the steeple.

Photo: A hovering angel wing near St. Germaine Catholic Church in Prescott Valley, Arizona on December 6th, 2020.

Photo: Another amazing hovering set of angel wings above Prescott Valley, Arizona on December 6th, 2020.

Photo: On December 6th, 2020 this amazing hovering angel face appeared above Prescott Valley, Arizona.

Photo: On December 8th, 2020 an amazing sequence of angel sightings followed by an amazing sunset took place. You can see this enormous angel forming above Prescott Valley, Arizona with a green orb to the right. It is breathtaking.

Photo: On December 8th, 2020 above Prescott Valley, Arizona this amazing image appeared of what looks like an angel face to the right biting down on the tail of another angel to the left.

Photo: On December 8th, 2020 while driving to work near Phoenix, Arizona to work with local retina surgeons this hovering "choir of angels" appeared to line the skies.

Photo: The evening of December 8th, 2020 near Prescott Valley, Arizona shows this incredible red hued sunset suggesting St. Mary is nearby and at work.

Photo: The sunset of December 11th, 2020 was incredibly supernatural. I can clearly see a horned demonic looking figure in the middle of the frame as if it is being exorcised off of the earth by the angels of light.

Photo: On December 13th, 2020 this incredibly beautiful angel feathered wing appeared above Prescott Valley, Arizona.

Photo: On December 13th, 2020 this incredibly beautiful angel face and wing appeared above Prescott Valley, Arizona.

Photo: On December 13th, 2020 this incredibly beautiful hovering angel with two wings appeared above Prescott Valley, Arizona.

Photo: The morning of December 14th, 2020 near Phoenix, Arizona took my breath away as this beautiful orange and red feathered wing hovered in the sky as I made my way to work with local retina surgeons.

Photo: An incredibly beautiful angel formation above Phoenix, Arizona on December 14th, 2020.

Photo: An incredibly beautiful angel formation above Phoenix, Arizona on December 14th, 2020.

Photo: An incredibly beautiful angel formation above Phoenix, Arizona on December 14th, 2020.

Photo: An incredibly beautiful angel formation above Phoenix, Arizona on December 14th, 2020.

Photo: An incredibly beautiful angel formation above Tucson, Arizona on December 14th, 2020.

Photo: December 17th, 2020 bore witness to this amazingly beautiful and huge angel wing above Tucson, Arizona where I was working with local retina surgeons and assisting in visualization during surgery.

Photo: The year 2021 started off with amazing angel views above St. Germaine Catholic Church in Prescott Valley, Arizona on January 2nd, 2021.

Photo: The year 2021 started off with amazing angel views above St. Germaine Catholic Church in Prescott Valley, Arizona on January 2nd, 2021. This appears to be a large set of wings.

Photo: The year 2021 started off with amazing angel views above St. Germaine Catholic Church in Prescott Valley, Arizona on January 2nd, 2021. This is a huge angel wing covering the entire sky.

Photo: The year 2021 started off with amazing angel views above St. Germaine Catholic Church in Prescott Valley, Arizona on January 2nd, 2021. This is another huge angel wing covering the entire sky.

Photo: The year 2021 started off with amazing angel views above St. Germaine Catholic Church in Prescott Valley, Arizona on January 2nd, 2021. This is another huge angel wing covering the entire sky.

Photo: On January 4th, 2021 this amazing angel wing appeared above our neighborhood in Prescott Valley, Arizona.

Photo: On January 8th, 2021 this amazing angel face appeared in the skies above Prescott Valley, Arizona. You can clearly see a large face with a horn hanging down on the left side of the face.

Photo: On January 8th, 2021 this amazing figure of a lion head with open mouth facing to the right appeared above our neighborhood in Prescott Valley, Arizona.

Photo: An amazingly beautiful angel feather wing appeared above Prescott Valley, Arizona on January 10th, 2021.

Photo: On January 10th, 2021 this amazing angel wing appeared above Prescott Valley, Arizona.

Photo: On January 10th, 2021 a single angel hovered over Prescott Valley, Arizona.

Photo: On January 10th, 2021 an incredible feathered wing appeared above Prescott Valley, Arizona.

Photo: On January 13th, 2021 this amazing image of a large pink angel appeared above Prescott Valley, Arizona. You can clearly see a large face with eyes to the bottom right of the frame.

Photo: On January 13th, 2021 a huge angel wing covered the skies above Prescott Valley, Arizona. You can see the American flag in the bottom right of the frame.

Photo: On January 13th, 2021 these amazing pair of hovering angel wings appeared above Prescott Valley, Arizona.

Photo: On January 13th, 2021 this incredible image of a flying angel to the left can be seen. There are two horns on its head.

Photo: On January 13th, 2021 you can see this amazing image of an angel flying arms outstretched towards the left.

Photo: One of the most beautiful sunsets I've ever seen on the evening of January 13th, 2021 near Prescott Valley, Arizona.

Photo: On the morning of January 16th, 2021 this amazing image appeared at sunrise while on the way to St. Germaine Catholic Church in Prescott Valley, Arizona to recite a full rosary for world peace and for the world to turn away from greed. You can clearly see an angel wing to the right of the sun and a beautiful pink/red and blue/green orb as the sun's rays streak towards the church.

Photo: A beautiful large feathered angel wing above the skies of Prescott Valley, Arizona on January 16th, 2021.

Photo: The morning of January 17th, 2021 near St. Germaine Catholic Church in Prescott Valley, Arizona as I entered the grounds to recite a full rosary for world peace and for the world to turn away from greed this amazing funneling angel wing shot straight up right above a stainless window showing Jesus Christ praying to heaven.

Photo: The morning of January 18th, 2021 bore witness to one of the most amazing sunrises I have ever seen in person. This is above Watson Lake near Prescott, Arizona. It appears as angels in flight on fire. It is breathtakingly beautiful.

Photo: On January 18th, 2021 shows another shot of the sunrise near Prescott Valley, Arizona. This appears like a huge angel wing on fire covering the entire sky. I was on my way for a morning rosary for world peace and for the world to turn away from war and greed.

Photo: An amazing image of a flying angel right above my rooftop the morning of January 18th, 2021 in Prescott Valley, Arizona. I had just recited a full rosary for world peace and for the world to turn away from war and greed.

Photo: An amazing image of a flying angel the morning of January 18th, 2021 in Prescott Valley, Arizona. I had just recited a full rosary for world peace and for the world to turn away from war and greed. You can clearly see two enormous angel wings covering the entire sky.

Photo: An amazing image of a flying angel the morning of January 18th, 2021 in Prescott Valley, Arizona. I had just recited a full rosary for world peace and for the world to turn away from war and greed. You can clearly see an enormous angel wing covering the entire sky.

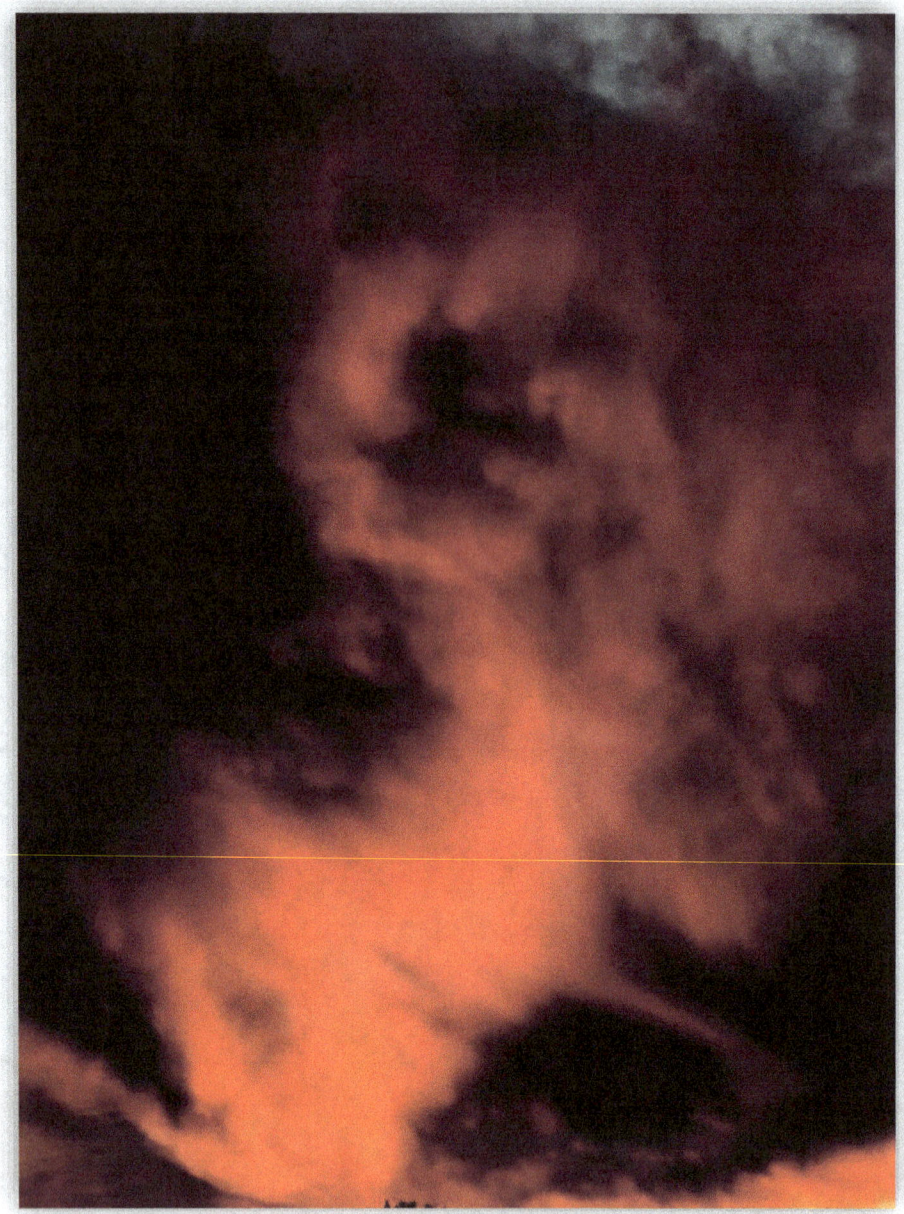

Photo: On January 18th, 2021 another amazing sunset was spotted in the skies above Prescott Valley, Arizona.

Photo: Another view of the amazingly beautiful sunset near Prescott Valley, Arizona on January 18th, 2021. I would definitely describe this sunset as very paranormal.

Photo: On January 19th, 2021 while in Las Vegas, Nevada working with retinal surgeons this amazingly beautiful and huge angel appeared above Sin City covering the entire sky.

Photo: On January 21st, 2021 while working in Las Vegas, Nevada with retinal surgeons this incredibly huge angel wing appeared in this skies after asking St. Michael to guard me in Sin City. If you look closely to the left leading edge of the wing you can almost see what appears to be the face of a pig. It reminds me of one of my favorite Pink Floyd songs "Pigs on the Wings" from the album Animals.

Photo: On January 23rd, 2021 this amazing photograph shows what appears to be two kissing angels in the skies above Prescott Valley, Arizona.

Photo: On January 23rd, 2021 above St. Germaine Catholic Church in Prescott Valley, Arizona this amazing angel wing appeared above the church right before a mass.

Photo: On January 27th, 2021 above Prescott Valley, Arizona this incredible angelic image appeared which looks like the head of a deer or heart to me.

Photo: On January 27th, 2021 above Prescott Valley, Arizona this incredible "choir of angels" appeared above our neighborhood after an unusual snowfall.

Photo: On January 27th, 2021 this incredible image of an angel screeching across the skies below the sun could be seen above Prescott Valley, Arizona.

Photo: On January 28th, 2021 this incredible hovering angel can be seen with what looks like two distinct faces above it near Prescott Valley, Arizona.

Photo: On January 28th, 2021 after a heavy snowfall in Prescott Valley, Arizona this incredible image of a large angel face between wings could be seen directly above our roof.

Photo: On January 28th, 2021 after a heavy snowfall in Prescott Valley, Arizona this incredible image of a large angel face between wings could be seen directly above our neighborhood.

Photo: On January 28th, 2021 after a heavy snowfall in Prescott Valley, Arizona this incredible image of a large risen demonic face with horns and its tongue sticking out could be seen directly above our neighborhood.

Photo: By far one of the most amazing photos I've ever captured of a hovering angel looking up towards heaven to the right could be seen directly above Prescott, Arizona on January 28th, 2021 after a heavy snowfall.

Photo: On January 28th, 2021 an incredible photograph of a an angel diving down to the left could be seen directly above Prescott, Arizona after a heavy snowfall.

Photo: On January 28th, 2021 another incredible photograph of a an angel flying to the left could be seen directly above Prescott, Arizona after a heavy snowfall.

Photo: On January 28th, 2021 an incredible photograph of a an angel holding up a cloud and flying to the left could be seen directly above Prescott, Arizona after a heavy snowfall.

Photo: On January 28th, 2021 an incredible photograph of a an angel hovering in place could be seen directly above Prescott, Arizona after a heavy snowfall. There is a very mysterious looking face near the top of the frame.

Photo: Another amazing angel in flight on January 28th, 2021 near Prescott Valley, Arizona after a heavy snowfall.

Photo: An incredible image of a hovering angel above Prescott Valley, Arizona on January 31st, 2021.

Photo: An incredible image of a hovering angel wing above Prescott Valley, Arizona on January 31st, 2021.

Photo: An incredible image of a hovering angel wing above a local church in Prescott Valley, Arizona on January 31st, 2021.

Photo: An incredible image of a hovering angel above Prescott Valley, Arizona on January 31st, 2021. If you look closely, you can see its wings are stretched out and its face gazing up towards heaven.

Photo: An incredible image of a hovering angel above Prescott Valley, Arizona on January 31st, 2021.

Photo: An incredible image of a hovering angel above Prescott Valley, Arizona on January 31st, 2021.

Photo: An incredible image of a hovering angel above Prescott Valley, Arizona on January 31st, 2021.

Photo: An incredible image of a hovering angel above Prescott, Arizona on January 31st, 2021 that came to protect my wife and I as we hiked Constellation Trail in Prescott, Arizona.

Photo: An incredible image of an angelic sunset above Prescott Valley, Arizona on January 31st, 2021. You can clearly see multiple faces in the setting sun.

Photo: An incredible event happened while in a hike in Sedona, Arizona on February 6th, 2021 with my wife Carol Rose Kloss (The New Rose). During the hike we found this peculiar rock in the shape of a heart. When we took the photo holding it together this amazing bending ray of sunlight passed directly through the heart shaped rock.

Photo: On February 7th, 2021 this incredibly huge angel wing appeared above Prescott Valley, Arizona.

Photo: On February 7th, 2021 this incredibly huge choir of angels appeared above Prescott Valley, Arizona. The beauty of this is difficult to comprehend.

Photo: On February 7th, 2021 this incredibly second huge choir of angels appeared above Prescott Valley, Arizona. The beauty of this is also difficult to comprehend.

Photo: On February 7th, 2021 this third incredibly huge choir of angels appeared above a local church in Prescott Valley, Arizona. The beauty of this is also difficult to comprehend.

Photo: On February 7th, 2021 this incredibly conflagration of angels appeared above Prescott Valley, Arizona. The beauty of this is difficult to comprehend.

Photo: On February 9th, 2021 this incredibly huge angel appeared above Prescott Valley, Arizona. The beauty of this is difficult to comprehend. Notice the lone bird flying near the top of the wing.

Photo: On February 9th, 2021 this incredibly huge angel appeared above Prescott Valley, Arizona.

Photo: On February 9th, 2021 this incredibly huge angel appeared above Prescott Valley, Arizona. The beauty of this is difficult to comprehend. Also notice a face in the middle of the frame.

Photo: On February 11th, 2021 this incredibly huge formation of angels appeared above Prescott Valley, Arizona. The beauty of this is difficult to comprehend. This is directly above my neighbor's rooftop.

Photo: On February 13th, 2021 this amazing image of two angel wings appeared above Prescott Valley, Arizona. The beauty of this is difficult to comprehend.

Photo: On February 13th, 2021 this stunning angel wing sunset appeared above Prescott Valley, Arizona. The beauty of this is difficult to comprehend.

Photo: On February 13th, 2021 this amazing image of enormous angel wings appeared above Prescott Valley, Arizona at sunset. This is one of the most stunning images I've ever captured.

Photo: On February 14th, 2021 this incredible blue angel appeared hovering over our neighborhood in Prescott Valley, Arizona. Notice the face in the top middle of the frame surrounded by multiple faces to the right of the frame.

Photo: On February 14th, 2021 this incredible hovering angel appeared over our neighborhood in Prescott Valley, Arizona.

Photo: On February 14th, 2021 this incredible angel appeared hovering over our neighborhood in Prescott Valley, Arizona.

Photo: On February 14th, 2021 this incredible angel appeared hovering over our neighborhood in Prescott Valley, Arizona.

Photo: On February 14th, 2021 this incredible angel appeared hovering over our neighborhood in Prescott Valley, Arizona.

Photo: On February 16th, 2021 this incredible blue angel appeared hovering over Phoenix, Arizona. If you look closely to the right side of the frame it appears as if it is bowing its head in prayer, wings folding behind him/her.

Photo: On February 17th, 2021 this stunning image was taken of low hanging clouds at sunset over the Mingus Mountains near our home in Prescott Valley, Arizona. This is one of the most beautiful images in nature I've ever captured.

Photo: On February 20th, 2021 this incredible sunset could be seen near our neighborhood in Prescott Valley, Arizona.

Photo: On February 23rd, 2021 this incredible set of angel wings appeared while driving to work assisting retina surgeons during surgery in Phoenix, Arizona.

Photo: On February 23rd, 2021 these angels appeared hovering over Phoenix, Arizona while one my way to work with retina surgeons during surgery.

Photo: On February 23rd, 2021 this enormously huge angel wing appeared hovering over Phoenix, Arizona while one my way to work with retina surgeons during surgery.

Photo: On February 23rd, 2021 this enormously huge angel wing appeared hovering over Phoenix, Arizona while one my way to work with retina surgeons during surgery.

Photo: On February 24th, 2021 this enormously huge angel wing appeared hovering over Prescott Valley, Arizona at sunset.

Photo: On February 26th, 2021 this enormously huge angel wing appeared hovering over Sedona, Arizona while visiting with family from out of state. This was my exact date of my birth and a beautiful present from the other kingdom.

Photo: On my birthday February 26th, 2021 I was able to spend some time with my amazing niece Priya, an angel from the other kingdom of heaven. You can see the bending angelic light that is protecting her and my wife Carol Rose (The New Rose).

Photo: On February 27th, 2021 this enormously huge angel appeared hovering over Sedona, Arizona while celebrating my birthday with family. The protection I felt from this appearance was overwhelming.

Photo: Protective angels on March 1st, 2021 above Prescott Valley, Arizona as I had family members visiting from out of town.

THE FALLEN NINETEEN

On March 2nd, 2021 my sister Kate and her four-year-old daughter Priya who was introduced in the last volume of **'The New Wine'** as being a special child from the other kingdom visited us in Arizona.

We went to see the memorial in Yarnell, Arizona of the fallen nineteen firefighters who died in 2013 fighting a wildfire near Yarnell. The event was dramatized in the movie "Only the Brave."

After we visited the memorial which was very emotional, driving home past a controlled burn near Prescott, Arizona something incredible occurred. There were multiple sightings of angels hovering as if in protection. I truly believe these were the angelic spirits of the nineteen firefighters still protecting us from beyond.

Photo: An incredible photo of hovering angels over a controlled burn near Prescott, Arizona on March 2nd, 2021. I believe these are the angels of the departed Hot Shot firefighters who perished in a wildfire in 2013 in nearby Yarnell, Arizona. Notice the green orb in the bottom of the frame signaling one with nature.

Photo: Another incredible photo of hovering angels over a controlled burn near Prescott, Arizona on March 2nd, 2021. I believe these are the angels of the departed Hot Shot firefighters who perished in a wildfire in 2013 in nearby Yarnell, Arizona.

Photo: Another incredible photo of hovering angels over a controlled burn near Prescott, Arizona on March 2nd, 2021. I believe these are the angels of the departed Hot Shot firefighters who perished in a wildfire in 2013 in nearby Yarnell, Arizona.

Photo: Another incredible photo of hovering angels over a controlled burn near Prescott, Arizona on March 2nd, 2021. I believe these are the angels of the departed Hot Shot firefighters who perished in a wildfire in 2013 in nearby Yarnell, Arizona.

Photo: An incredible photo of a hovering angel over a controlled burn near Prescott, Arizona on March 2nd, 2021. I believe these are the angels of the departed Hot Shot firefighters who perished in a wildfire in 2013 in nearby Yarnell, Arizona.

Photo: An incredible photo of a hovering angel over a controlled burn near Prescott, Arizona on March 2nd, 2021. I believe this is actually one of the seven horses on the mark of the Apocalypse as prophesied in the Doors song "Love Her Madly."

Photo: An incredible image of an angel hovering over my niece Priya on March 3rd, 2021 near our home in Prescott Valley, Arizona.

Photo: An incredible image of an angel flying sideways on March 3rd, 2021 near Prescott Valley, Arizona.

Photo: A beautiful set of angel wings on March 3rd, 2021 near Prescott Valley, Arizona

Photo: An incredible shot of hovering angels on March 6th, 2021 near Prescott Valley, Arizona.

Photo: Another incredible shot of hovering angels on March 6th, 2021 near Prescott Valley, Arizona.

Photo: Another incredible shot of hovering angels on March 6th, 2021 near Prescott Valley, Arizona.

Photo: Another incredible shot of a hovering angel on March 6th, 2021 near Prescott, Arizona above Sacred Heart Catholic Church.

Photo: Another incredible shot of a hovering angel on March 6th, 2021 near Prescott Valley, Arizona.

Photo: Another incredible shot of a hovering angel on March 6th, 2021 near Prescott Valley, Arizona.

Photo: Another incredible shot of a hovering angel on March 6th, 2021 near Prescott Valley, Arizona.

Photo: Another incredible shot of a hovering angel on March 6th, 2021 near Prescott Valley, Arizona.

Photo: Another incredible shot of a hovering angel on March 6th, 2021 near Prescott Valley, Arizona.

Photo: Another incredible shot of a hovering angel on March 6th, 2021 near Prescott Valley, Arizona.

Photo: Another incredible shot of hovering angels on March 6th, 2021 near Prescott Valley, Arizona.

Photo: Another incredible shot of a hovering angel on March 6th, 2021 near Prescott Valley, Arizona. You can see the cross below the angel from a local Christian church.

Photo: Another incredible shot of angels in flight on March 6th, 2021 near Prescott Valley, Arizona.

Photo: Another incredible shot of hovering angels on March 6th, 2021 near Prescott Valley, Arizona. You can clearly see two faces in the wing.

Photo: Another incredible shot of hovering angels on March 6th, 2021 near Prescott Valley, Arizona.

Photo: An incredible shot of hovering angels on March 6th, 2021 near Prescott Valley, Arizona at sunset.

Photo: A beautiful radiant sunset on March 6th, 2021 near Prescott Valley, Arizona.

Photo: An incredible shot of a hovering angel directly above my hotel in Salt Lake City, Utah on March 11th, 2021 while working with local retina surgeons assisting in visualization during surgery.

Photo: An incredible shot of a blue angel hovering in the middle of a white angel wing cloud formation. It appears as if this angel is going for a ride.

Photo: An incredible shot of an angel hovering above Salt Lake City, Utah on March 15th, 2021 while working with local retina surgeons in surgery.

Photo: A radiant sunset above Prescott Valley, Arizona on March 16th, 2021

Photo: An incredible shot of an angel in flight above Prescott Valley, Arizona on St. Patrick's Day March 17th, 2021.

Photo: A beautiful angel in flight above Prescott Valley, Arizona on March 18th, 2021. You can clearly see the face in the middle of the frame.

Photo: Angels hovering above Sacred Heart Catholic Church in Prescott, Arizona on March 20th, 2021 while on my way in to recite a rosary for world peace and for the world to turn away from war and greed.

Photo: A beautiful set of angel wings above Prescott, Arizona on March 20th, 2021.

Photo: Another beautiful set of angel wings above Prescott, Arizona on March 20th, 2021.

Photo: A beautiful angel wing above Sacred Heart Catholic Church in Prescott, Arizona on March 20th, 2021 while visiting to recite a rosary for world peace and for the world to turn away from war and greed.

Photo: A huge angel hovering above Prescott, Arizona on March 20th, 2021. You can see a face in the middle near the sun with a rainbow halo and green orb.

Photo: A beautiful and huge angel wing above Prescott Valley, Arizona on March 20th, 2021.

Photo: An incredible image of a flying angel above Prescott Valley, Arizona on March 22nd, 2021. You can clearly see a face in the middle surrounded by beautiful flowing wings.

Photo: An incredible image of flying angels above Prescott Valley, Arizona on March 22nd, 2021.

Photo: An incredible shot of a flying angel above Prescott Valley, Arizona on March 22nd, 2021. You can clearly see the face in the middle with arms/wings outstretched.

Photo: An incredible shot of a flying angel above Prescott Valley, Arizona on March 24th, 2021. You can clearly see the face in the middle with arms/wings outstretched and green orb.

Photo: A huge angel wing above Las Vegas, Nevada on March 24th, 2021 while working with local retina surgeons assisting with visualization during surgery.

Photo: An incredible glimpse of the other kingdom of heaven from the angels in March 25th, 2021 near Chino Valley, Arizona.

Photo: An amazing angel hovering above our neighborhood in Prescott Valley, Arizona on March 27th, 2021. Notice the radiant blue halo around the sun and the blue/green orb near the bottom of the frame.

Photo: A beautiful angel wing above our home in Prescott Valley, Arizona on March 27th, 2021. You can see many angels and faces with feathered wings in the frame.

Photo: A huge blue angel face directly above our roof in Prescott Valley, Arizona on March 27th, 2021. You can see a face with eyes in the middle with wings behind the face.

Photo: Two huge angel faces above our home on March 27th, 2021 near Prescott Valley, Arizona.

Photo: A huge angel hovering above our neighborhood on March 27th, 2021. You can see a face in the middle of the frame.

Photo: A huge angel hovering above Prescott Valley, Arizona on March 29th, 2021. You can see a face in the middle of the frame.

Photo: A beautiful angelic sunset on March 29th, 2021 near Prescott Valley, Arizona.

Photo: Beautiful angels hovering above Prescott Valley, Arizona on March 30th, 2021 at sunset.

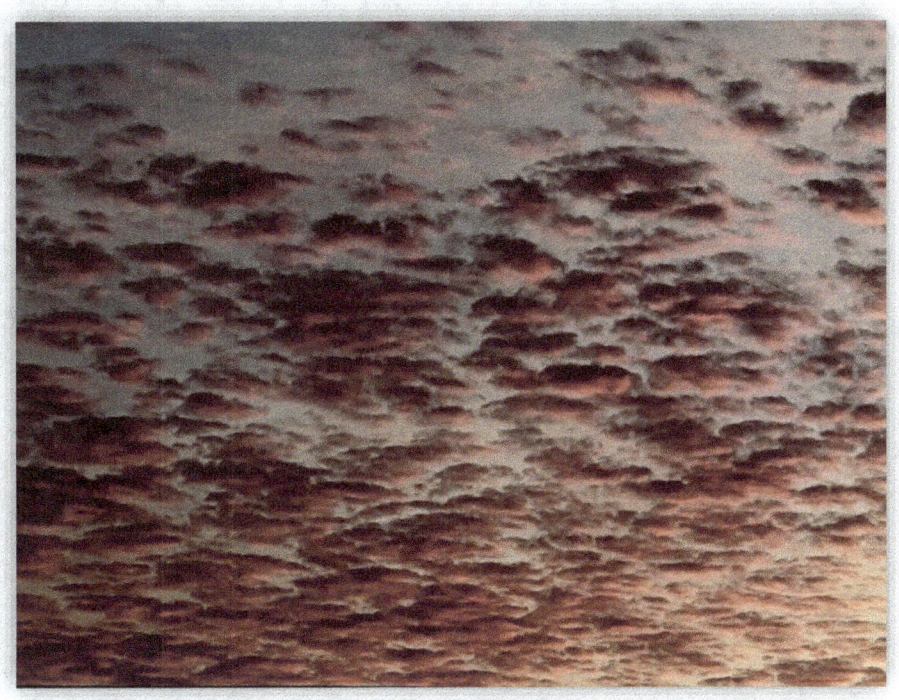

Photo: A beautiful angelic sunrise the morning of April Fool's Day April 1st, 2021 above Prescott Valley, Arizona.

Photo: A beautiful angelic sunrise the morning of April Fool's Day April 1st, 2021 above Prescott Valley, Arizona. This huge wing covering the sky was such an amazing feeling of total power and energy from on high.

Photo: A beautiful angelic sunrise the morning of April Fool's Day April 1st, 2021 above Prescott Valley, Arizona. This huge wing covering the sky was such an amazing feeling of total power and energy from on high. There is also a blue/green orb near the bottom middle of the frame.

Photo: A beautiful and huge angel wing above Prescott Valley, Arizona on April 1st, 2021 after a morning rosary for the world to turn away from war and greed.

Photo: A beautiful and huge angel wing above Prescott Valley, Arizona on April 2nd, 2021 after a morning rosary for the world to turn away from war and greed. Notice the blue/green orb to the right of the frame.

Photo: An incredibly beautiful sunset above Prescott Valley, Arizona on April 2nd, 2021.

Photo: A beautiful huge wing behind our backyard in Prescott Valley, Arizona on April 3rd, 2021

Photo: An incredible angel above Prescott Valley, Arizona on April 4th, 2021. You can clearly see a face on the top right of the frame that looks like a dog's face to me.

Photo: An incredible angel above Prescott Valley, Arizona on April 4th, 2021.

Photo: Another incredible angel wing above Prescott Valley, Arizona on April 5th, 2021.

Photo: A beautiful angelic sunset in Prescott Valley, Arizona on April 6th, 2021. The wing is unmistakable

Photo: Another morphing shot of a beautiful angelic sunset in Prescott Valley, Arizona on April 6th, 2021. The wing is unmistakable.

Photo: An incredible angel of protection directly above my hotel in Logan, Utah on April 7th, 2021 and I visited local retina surgeons to assist with visualization during surgery.

Photo: Another incredible angel of protection directly above my hotel in Logan, Utah on April 7th, 2021 and I visited local retina surgeons to assist with visualization during surgery.

Photo: An incredible shot of angels hovering above Salt Lake City, Utah on April 10th, 2021 as I worked with local retina surgeons assisting in visualization during surgery.

Photo: An incredible shot of huge angel hovering above Salt Lake City, Utah on April 10th, 2021 as I worked with local retina surgeons assisting in visualization during surgery.

Photo: Another incredible shot of an angel hovering above Salt Lake City, Utah on April 10th, 2021 as I worked with local retina surgeons assisting in visualization during surgery.

Photo: An incredible shot of angels hovering above Prescott Valley, Arizona on April 11th, 2021.

Photo: An incredible shot of angels hovering above Prescott Valley, Arizona on April 11th, 2021.

Photo: An incredible shot of angels hovering above Prescott Valley, Arizona on April 11th, 2021.

Photo: An incredible shot of angels hovering above Prescott Valley, Arizona on April 11th, 2021. Notice the multi-colored orbs and halos.

Photo: An incredible shot of angels hovering above Prescott Valley, Arizona on April 12th, 2021.

Photo: An incredible shot of angels hovering above Prescott Valley, Arizona on April 12th, 2021.

Photo: An incredible shot of angels hovering above Prescott Valley, Arizona on April 12th, 2021.

Photo: An incredible shot of angels hovering above Prescott Valley, Arizona on April 12th, 2021.

Photo: An incredible shot of a huge angel face hovering above Prescott Valley, Arizona on April 15th, 2021.

Photo: A beautiful angel wing hovering above Prescott Valley, Arizona on April

16th, 2021.

Photo: A beautiful angel wing hovering above Prescott Valley, Arizona on April 16th, 2021.

Photo: A beautiful row of angels hovering above Prescott Valley, Arizona on April 16th, 2021.

Photo: Two huge angel faces hovering above Prescott Valley, Arizona on April 16th, 2021. Do you see them smiling?

Photo: A beautiful angel wing sunset on April 16th, 2021 above our neighborhood in Prescott Valley, Arizona.

Photo: A beautiful huge kneeling blue angel above Prescott Valley, Arizona on April 17th, 2021.

Photo: A huge angel wing above our neighborhood in April 17th, 2021.

AN EXORCISING SUNSET

The evening of April 17th, 2021 bore witness to one of the most paranormal sunsets I've ever seen.

The photos below were taken in sequence and show what appears to be multiple demonic faces being exorcised from the earth. I am taking this as a tremendously positive sign for the world.

Photo: The sunset on April 17th, 2021 began with this strange low hanging orange curtain above Prescott Valley, Arizona.

Photo: A strange looking face in the clouds above Prescott Valley, Arizona on April 17th, 2021.

Photo: Multiple demonic looking faces appear at sunset in Prescott Valley, Arizona on April 17th, 2021.

Photo: Multiple demonic looking faces appear at sunset in Prescott Valley, Arizona on April 17th, 2021.

Photo: Multiple demonic looking faces appear at sunset in Prescott Valley, Arizona on April 17th, 2021.

Photo: Multiple demonic looking faces seem to morph into one large angry demon that appeared at sunset in Prescott Valley, Arizona on April 17th, 2021.

Photo: Multiple demonic looking faces seem to morph into one large angry demon that appeared at sunset in Prescott Valley, Arizona on April 17th, 2021.

Photo: You can clearly see multiple faces in the sunset here on April 20th, 2021 above Prescott Valley, Arizona.

Photo: You can clearly see multiple faces in the sunset here on April 20th, 2021 above Prescott Valley, Arizona.

Photo: A huge angel wing covers the skies above Prescott Valley, Arizona on April 22nd, 2021.

Photo: An incredible image of a "soldier angel" above Prescott Valley, Arizona on April 23rd, 2021. You can see an incredible helmet like what a Roman soldier might wear into battle.

Photo: On April 26th, 2021 incredible images of huge feathered wing angels hovering above Prescott Valley, Arizona.

Photo: On April 26th, 2021 incredible images of huge feathered wing angel faces hovering above Prescott Valley, Arizona.

Photo: On April 26th, 2021 incredible images of huge feathered wing angels hovering above Prescott Valley, Arizona with a blue/green orb to the bottom left of the frame.

Photo: On April 26th, 2021 incredible images of huge feathered wing angels hovering above Prescott Valley, Arizona with another blue/green orb in the middle of the frame.

Photo: On April 26th, 2021 incredible images of huge feathered wing angels hovering above Prescott Valley, Arizona.

Photo: On April 26th, 2021 incredible images of huge feathered wing angels hovering above Prescott Valley, Arizona.

Photo: Two enormous angel faces above Prescott Valley, Arizona on April 27th, 2021.

Photo: An ominous cloud above Prescott Valley, Arizona on April 17th, 2021 after morning rosary prayers for world peace. I found this cloud ominous because to me it looks like the mushroom cloud from a nuclear explosion. With what is occurring the Middle East and with Russia and China threatening borders this world must be mindful of the drastic consequences of waging such an unwinnable confrontation.

Photo: An incredible view of angels hovering above our neighborhood in Prescott Valley, Arizona on April 29th, 2021. You can see multiple faces in the clouds filled with feathered wings.

Photo: An enormous angel face looking to the left above the skies in Prescott Valley, Arizona on April 28th, 2021.

Photo: An enormous angel wing hovers in protection over St. Germaine Catholic Church in Prescott Valley, Arizona on April 28th, 2021.

Photo: An incredible radiant sunset above Prescott Valley, Arizona on April 30th, 2021.

Photo: An incredible radiant sunset above Prescott Valley, Arizona on April 30th, 2021 shows multiple angel faces staring down from above.

Photo: More beautiful angels in the skies above Prescott, Arizona on May 1st, 2021.

Photo: A beautiful angel face looking to the right on May 1st, 2021.

Photo: A beautiful angel in flight on May 1st, 2021 above Prescott Valley, Arizona.

Photo: Another beautiful angel in flight on May 1st, 2021 above Prescott Valley, Arizona.

Photo: Another beautiful angel in flight on May 1st, 2021 above Prescott Valley, Arizona. You can see a cross in the middle of a blue kneeling angel.

Photo: Another beautiful angel in flight on May 1st, 2021 above Prescott, Arizona.

Photo: A heavenly sunset on May 2nd, 2021 above Prescott Valley, Arizona.

Photo: Another beautiful angel in flight above Prescott, Arizona on May 4th, 2021.

Photo: Another beautiful angel in flight above Prescott, Arizona on May 4th, 2021.

Photo: Another incredible view of angels in flight above Prescott Valley, Arizona on May 6th, 2021.

Photo: Another incredible view of angels in flight above Prescott Valley, Arizona on May 6th, 2021.

Photo: Another incredible view of angels in flight above Prescott Valley, Arizona on May 6th, 2021.

Photo: Another incredible view of angels in flight above Prescott Valley,

Photo: Another incredible view of angels in flight above Prescott Valley,

Photo: An incredible angel wing sunset above Prescott Valley, Arizona on May 7th, 2021.

Photo: Beautiful angels hovering above Tucson, Arizona on May 13th, 2021 while working with local retina surgeons assisting with visualization during retina surgery. This was the 104th Anniversary of the Fatima Apparitions of St. Mary to farm children in Spain.

Photo: Beautiful angels hovering above Tucson, Arizona on May 13th, 2021 while working with local retina surgeons assisting with visualization during retina surgery.

Photo: Beautiful angels hovering above Tucson, Arizona on May 13th, 2021 while working with local retina surgeons assisting with visualization during retina surgery.

Photo: Beautiful angels hovering above Tucson, Arizona on May 13th, 2021 while working with local retina surgeons assisting with visualization during retina surgery.

Photo: Beautiful angels hovering above Tucson, Arizona on May 13th, 2021 while working with local retina surgeons assisting with visualization during retina surgery.

Photo: Beautiful angels hovering above Tucson, Arizona on May 13th, 2021 while working with local retina surgeons assisting with visualization during retina surgery.

Photo: A beautiful angel wing covering Prescott Valley, Arizona on May 15th, 2021.

Photo: A huge angel face above the skies near Prescott Valley, Arizona on May 17th, 2021.

Photo: A beautiful angelic cloud above Prescott Valley, Arizona on May 17th, 2021. Do you see the cross-top left?

Photo: A huge angel wing above Prescott Valley, Arizona on May 18th, 2021. You can see a blue/green orb in left of the frame.

Photo: An absolutely stunning sunset on May 18th, 2021 above Prescott Valley, Arizona.

Photo: A beautiful feathered wing above New River, Arizona on May 19th, 2021.

Photo: A huge angel wing above Black Canyon City, Arizona on May 19th, 2021.

Photo: While in my way to recite a full rosary at St. Germaine Catholic Church in Prescott Valley, Arizona this amazingly beautiful angel wing appeared directly above the church grounds.

Photo: A stunningly beautiful angel wing above Prescott Valley, Arizona on May 20th, 2021.

Photo: On a drive near Sedona, Arizona these incredible set of angel wings appeared on May 20th, 2021.

Photo: On a drive near Sedona, Arizona these incredible set of angel wings appeared on May 20th, 2021.

Photo: On a drive near Sedona, Arizona these incredible set of angel wings appeared on May 20th, 2021.

Photo: On a drive near Sedona, Arizona these incredible set of angel wings appeared on May 20th, 2021.

Photo: The incredible sunset of May 20th, 2021 shows a cross in the clouds above Prescott Valley, Arizona.

Photo: The incredible sunset of May 20th, 2021 shows a cross in the clouds above Prescott Valley, Arizona

Photo: These incredible set of angel wings appeared on May 21st, 2021 above Prescott Valley, Arizona after a morning rosary for world peace and for the world to turn away from war and greed.

Photo: This incredible angel wing appeared the morning of May 21st, 2021 above Prescott Valley, Arizona after a morning rosary for world peace and for the world to turn away from war and greed.

Photo: An incredible angel wing at sunrise near Prescott Valley, Arizona on May 21st, 2021 while on my way to St. Germaine Catholic Church for a morning rosary for world peace and for the world to turn away from war and greed.

SENDING ANGELS TO NEW FRIENDS

I recently joined an Angel Group on Facebook that has proven to be quite an amazing group of angels on earth. Many folks are looking for higher spiritual experiences in this fallen and often desolate world.

Two stories, I shared of an amazing involvement with angles with members named Tamara and Diane. I first came across a request on line on the Facebook Group by Tamara requesting psychic assistance for a serious family issue.

We connected over the phone and discussed a situation in which Tamara believed that a family member was in danger from a very powerful negative spiritual attack in their home. I assured Tamara in my ability to help.

On March 23rd, 2021 I started some morning prayers. I also specifically requested that St. Mary send powerful Arch Angels to Tamara and her sister Julie and the Tampa, Florida area.

Tamara said that she would look for the angels I promised as she drove to her sister's house in the Tampa area. The drive revealed numerous angels hovering in the sky.

Photo: A beautiful photo of a huge blue angel walking in the skies above the Tampa Bay, Florida area on March 23rd, 2021 after praying with an angel friend named Tamara who requested spiritual assistance for a family member. This sight was amazing and comforting to us both.

Photo: On March 23rd, 2021 as an angel friend named Tamara entered her sister's neighborhood to try to cleanse the home of negative spiritual entities this incredible single angel wing feather could be seen floating near a cloud.

Photo: Another amazing photo of a hovering blue cross directly above an angel friend named Tamara onMarch23rd, 2021 after prayers of deliverance for the home to be freed of negative energies. This sight was amazing and after I had said prayers the same morning for St. Mary to send Tamara and her family angels as protection.

Photo: An amazing photograph from April of 2021 sent to me from an angel friend named Tamara whose sister's home we cleansed of negative fallen spiritual energies. Tamara sent me this amazing photo of two golden pillars above Tampa Bay, Florida. I told her I believed that it means that St. Mary is saying she and her sister are now viewed as golden pillars of spiritual power over the fallen angels.

Photo: Another photo sent to me of my angel friend Tamara walking on the beach near Tampa Bay, Florida approximately three years before we met and I was able to assist her sister of cleansing negative fallen energies from her home in early 2021. I told Tamara I see the face of Jesus Christ directly above her near the top of the frame. It looks as if he was guiding her then and we were supposed to meet.

ANGELS SENT

The next story, is about an angel friend named Diane Douglas Leckel. Diane has become quite a loyal fan of **'The New Wine'**, book series.

In April 2021, she asked if I could send angels to her in North Andover, Massachusetts. On April 21st, 2021 I said my usual full rosary at St. Germaine Catholic Church in Prescott Valley, Arizona and asked St. Mary to send Diane angels within the next three days. Diane messaged me on April 23rd, 2021 to say many angels had been visiting and she had some amazing photographs to share.

Photo: A huge blue angel hovering over my angel friend Diane Douglass Leckel near her home in North Andover, Massachusetts on April 23rd, 2021 only three days after I said prayers for St. Mary to send angels to Diane.

Photo: An enormous angel face to the top right of the frame on April 23rd, 2021 as they visited my new angel friend and supporter of The New Wine books Diane Douglas Leckel.

Photo: Another enormous angel face to the top middle of the frame on April 23rd, 2021 as they visited my new angel friend and supporter of The New Wine books Diane Douglas Leckel.

Photo: An enormous angel wing cloud to the top left of the frame on April 23rd, 2021 as they visited my new angel friend and supporter of The New Wine books Diane Douglas Leckel as she drove through town in North Andover, Massachusetts. This is amazing proof that angels do exist and we can call on them through prayer to assist us and visit others for protection.

Photo: This amazing photograph was shared with me by my new angel friend Diane Douglass Leckel of the day her sister passed away in 2018. Diane believed that this angel was present to bring her sister's spirit to heaven.

Photo: An amazing photo of what appears to me as a demonic looking face looking to the right with two horns on its head. My new angel friend Diane Douglass Leckel shared this photo with me from the night of May 21st, 2021. I shared with Diane that I believed it was important for her to stay protected as the fallen angels/demons will hate my book series The New Wine as it is meant to bind them from interfering on earth. Demons are inherently attracted to the moon and the night. This one appears to be safely out of reach from Diane but nevertheless it is a chilling photograph.

AN EVER-APPROACHING APOCALYPSE

The Gospel of Matthew 24:6-8 NIV version states that Jesus told us prior to his second, "You will hear of wars and rumors of wars, but see to it that you are not alarmed. Such things must happen, but the end is still to come. Nation will rise up against nation, and kingdom against kingdom. There will be famines and earthquakes in various places."

All these are the beginnings of birth pains. Since the publication of **'The New Wine'** *Volume IV: Kingdom Come*, we have continued to witness an earthquake per day on the magnitude of 4.0 - 8.0 on the Richter scale.

There are too many to even keep count; in the event, you have doubts please search the information online.

We have seen major volcanic eruptions in late 2020 and early 2021.In particular, the volcanic eruption of Mt. Etna was a major eruption that lasted for weeks and appeared very apocalyptic in photographs. Another major eruption occurred that nearly engulfed the entire island of St. Vincent in the Caribbean.

The messages continue with massive wildfire that have engulfed much of the West Coast of the United States and many meteor streaks through our skies causing loud explosions.

One other sign, proves the massive floods hitting the southern states in early 2021.

Plus, the rare ice storm in Texas, February of 2021 that paralyzed the nation's largest state.

In terms of wars and rumors of wars, seen in 2021 like armed conflicts between Israel and Hamas that has resulted in many casualties. Another situation that appears to be building in Russian near the Ukraine border, also threatening moves by the People's Liberation Army of China towards Taiwan.

The events seem to align with Matthew 24:6-8.

Photo: An apocalyptic view of Mt. Etna in Italy continuously erupting in 2021

that appears like a "lake of fire."

Photo: Another shot of the massive and enduring explosion of Mt. Etna in Italy in 2021 that lasted for weeks on end.

Photo: Another amazing image of the massive eruption of Mt. Etna in Italy in early 2021. I circled what appears to me to be a demonic looking face in the erupting fire and ash.

Photo: Another massive volcanic eruption from Mt. Sinabung in Indonesia in March 2021 that appears quite apocalyptic in its appearance.

Photo: A major eruption of the volcano on the Caribbean Island of St. Vincent in April 2021 that left the island "unrecognizable" and caused millions of dollars of damage.

Photo: On May 22nd, 2021 a major eruption of a volcano in the Eastern Congo

left many residents trembling with fear. I see multiple demonic looking faces in the fire and ash here as w

Photo: An apocalyptic view of wildfires in late 2020 on the West Coast of The United States. The wildfires burned so greatly that they could be seen from outer space going far out into the Pacific Ocean.

Photo: A streaking meteor burns bright in the night skies above the St. Louis Arch in November of 2019 that appears quite apocalyptic.

Photo: Another streaking meteor above the skies near Puerto Rico in January 2020 appears rather apocalyptic.

Photo: A meteor explodes in a bright flame above Canada on February 22nd, 2021 in yet another apocalyptic type of image.

Photo: An amazing photograph of the super Pink Moon of April 26th, 2021. Many believe this pink moon brings fertility, change, and new spiritual growth to the world.

Photo: A beautiful photograph of the Orion Nebula, my second home and home to Annunaki Adonai, Annunaki Angels and St. Mary. This other kingdom will not abandon us in our time of need.

Photo: An artist rendering of the very unusual "space hurricane" we witnessed in early 2021 that brought many amazing views of the northern lights near the north pole.

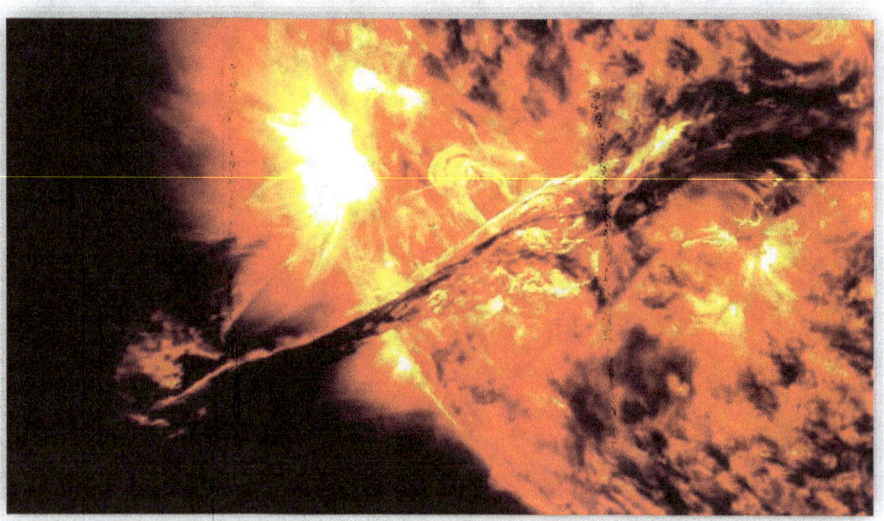

Photo: An artistic rendering of a massive "filament" solar flare exploding from our sun towards earth that brings with it major solar storms in early 2021

A rare ring of fire solar eclipse on June 10, 2021 saw an incredible twenty seven volcanoes erupt the following day.

Photo: A beautiful shot of the Northern lights in early 2021 from major fluctuations in magnetic activity on earth. I also believe his is evidence of the massive influx of angels appearing on earth coming through Einstein Rosen bridges from Heaven/Eden. A near the Nebula Orion to help us during this very difficult time on earth

Photo: An apocalyptic image of the iron dome anti-missile system being activated over Israel in response to a myriad of rockets being fired by Hamas soldiers to the right in early 2021 during a major confrontation in the Middle East. The photo looks like it is right out of a Sci-Fi movie.

THE DENVER INTERNATIONAL AIRPORT CONSPIRACY

I want to take a moment to discuss a widely held conspiracy theory that has interested me for many years. Many believe that the Denver International Airport is an Illuminati underground alien/reptilian/demonic military base that might be used to shelter the wealthy and elites in the event of a nuclear war or world ending pandemic.

I've seen recent shows where the host was allowed full access to all underground areas below the airport in an attempt to discredit the conspiracy theories. While all of this seemed convincing a recent visit, after a November in 2020 it further piqued my interest in the conspiracies. Since my suspicions were altered, walking through the airport, I happened to this a bizarre mural (which seemed very out of place for an international airport) of a demonic entity with wings.

Photo: A very bizarre and unsettling piece of artwork hanging in the Denver International Airport that I witnessed in November of 2020 while visiting with local retina surgeons to assist with visualization during retina surgery.

Photo: The "Blue Mustang" horse from the entrance to the Denver International Airport that many conspiracies theorize is an underground demonic alien/reptilian military base for the world Elites. The horse with red eyes does seem quite suggestive of satanic/demonic undertones.

Photo: This mural sits inside the Denver International Airport and it is quite unusual. We see a figure that looks like "death" or a soldier carrying an automatic weapon encircling child of the world. It is a very strange and bizarre piece of artwork and many have used this as further evidence of an ominous presence and agenda within the Denver Airport.

Photo: Another strange painting from inside the Denver International Airport shows what appears to be some kind of alien or God "re-seeding" the human race on earth with fertility, rebirth, etc. possibly following some kind of large-scale disaster which could be a nuclear or biological world war or pandemic. The artwork is quite bizarre for an airport I have to admit.

AN ANGEL IN MICHIGAN

One amazing story I want to share, in my opinion one of the most amazing angel sightings ever caught on camera.

On May 17th, 2018 Glen Thorman capture an image of a hovering angel floating above his pickup truck in Michigan. You can clearly see the angel's head; wings and it appears to be holding a flaming sword.

What's interesting about this sighting was it came exactly one year after Chris Cornell died in Detroit tragically following a concert.

I always suspected Chris' death had a supernatural component and was most likely, the result of an encounter with Lucifer. I believe Chris is also a Son of God and a Prophet as well.

Photo: An incredible photograph of a hovering angel flaming sword in hand taken by Glen Thurman in Michigan on May 17th, 2018. This might be on the clearest images of an angel caught on camera I have ever seen. It is very comforting.

Author's Note:

The angel sighting in Michigan,

> "Death makes angels of us all and gives us wings where we had shoulders smooth as raven's claws. Draw now your flaming swords angels and join this hunter of the green vest who has wrestled before with lions in the night."

At time people sometimes ask, "Why do I write these books?"

My answer is simple, "When I look at the dire current state of affairs, mankind seems to be teetering on the edge of total destruction. However, there is still magnificent beauty in our midst and an angel presence from the other kingdom that is bound by Our Father in Heaven to never forget or abandon us."

As examples, Tamara and Diane who now are absolute angel attractors themselves.

I write them in memory of Paxton Nathaniel Elkins, the young angelic boy whose amazing story kicked off this book series; will not be in vain.

I pray every day the world will wake up to certain realities and see connections to these apocalyptic events. These happenings occur, due to unending human (demonic) greed. The senseless wars are a way to fund their ravenousness gluttony.

My hope is to stir something deep within you, a passion you will share with as many people as you encounter in your life.

We can change the trajectory of this world, but we can only do it together. Remember the Devil works in deception and division. We win when we unite with one goal in mind and that is to fulfill the destiny our Great Creator envisioned for us all at birth. It is to be unending, eternal witnesses to the existence of the other kingdom.

May God Bless all of you who decided to read the entire book. The Kingdom of God resides within you, sanctifying the Precious Blood.

ABOUT THE Author

Matthew Douglas Pinard is the author of The New Wine series. He was born and raised in southeastern Michigan and has a bachelor's degree in psychology from the University of Michigan and a master's degree in military history from Louisiana State University. Matthew is also a former US Army JAG legal specialist. He and his wife Carol Rose are recent transplants from west Michigan and now live in beautiful Prescott Valley, Arizona, with their two dogs Reese, a chocolate Lab, and Cleetus, a Redbone Coonhound. Matthew is a ranked Shihan (sixth degree) in Hakko Den shin Ryu Japanese Jujutsu and enjoys hiking, communing with the other side, praying for world peace, and photographing archangels in his spare time.

OTHER BOOKS BY AUTHOR MATTHEW DOUGLAS PINARD

matthewpinardauthor.com

Follow Me:

- Goodreads
- Author Central
- YouTube

MATTHEW DOUGLAS PINARD

@matthewpinardauthor.com

SCREENPLAY AWARDS
MATTHEW DOUGLAS PINARD

Official Selection

- Bloodstained Indie Film Festival
- StoryPros Awards Screenplay Contest
- Military Script Showcase
- L.A. Neo Noir Novel Film & Script Festival
- True Story International Film Festival
- Reel Heart International Film Festival
- Hollywood Boulevard International Film Festival
- Independent Talents International Film Festival
- Fort Worth Indie Film Showcase
- California Independent Film Festival
- San Pedro International Film Festival,
- Southeastern International Film Festival
- Louisiana International Film Festival

Official Selection

- First Ten Pages Script Contest
- Atlanta Comedy Film Festival
- Georgia Shorts Film Festival

Official Finalist

- Las Vegas International Film and Screenwriting Contest,Honorable Mention
- Depth of Field International Film Festival, Award Winner
- Beverly Hills International Film Festival, Silver Winner
- Queen Palm International Film Festival, Award Winner

- [Colorado International Film Festival](), **Quarter-Finalist**
- [Chicago Screenplay Awards](), **Quarter-Finalist**
- [NYC International Screenplay Awards](), **Quarter-Finalist**
- [Atlanta Screenplay Awards](), Semi-Finalist
- [Cordillera International Film Festival](), Semi-Finalist
- [Fade In Awards](), **Finalist**
- [Breaking Walls Thriller Screenplay]() **Award Winner**
- [Vegas Movie Awards](),
- [The Santa Barbara International Screenplay Awards](), **Finalist**
- [Miami Screen Play Awards,]() **Quarter-Finalist:**

www.ingramcontent.com/pod-product-compliance
Lightning Source LLC
Chambersburg PA
CBHW081352070526
44583CB00020B/2531